YONDER

YONDER

Travelogues

Jack Oakley

URTEXT
San Rafael

Copyright ©2015 by Jack Oakley. All rights reserved. No part of this publication may be reproduced, stored in a retrieval system or transmitted in any form or by any means, electronic, mechanical, photocopying, recording, or otherwise, without the prior written permission of the copyright holder, except brief quotations used in a review.

Book and cover design by Glenn Claycomb.

ISBN: 978-1-940121-07-9

Published by Urtext
San Rafael, California
www.urtext.us

Printed in the United States of America

Contents

Marrakech	7
Wanderlust	8
Scars	10
The Dentimale	12
The Askiyan Revolution	13
In the Royal Tombs of Ur	15
In the Royal Tombs of Egypt's Old Kingdom	18
The Cappadocian Cave Network	19
Négresse Station (Biarritz)	20
Langon	25
Saint Macaire	27
Bordeaux to Denver	36
Gran Canaria	43
Southward	52
Down the River to Manaus	72
Harbin	79
The Getty Museum in LA	110
To Idaho with my Son	112
Paris in 2005	113
A Few Days in Umbria with the Family	114
Tehran 2005	121
The New California Academy of Sciences Museum	137
A Couple Days in San Diego	142

Marrakech

There is a crumbling wall surrounding old Marrakech, a massive earthen rampart three stories tall which bakes in the hot cloudless days on the edge of the desert. The Atlas range rises snowless from the depths of a distant depression. A dirt path wide enough for one of the rare automobiles runs beside the wall. Men and women walk along making a tour of the city or turn into one of the keyhole entrances or randomly away to disappear into the thick and thorny brush which pushes up like kelp from the bottom of a dusty ocean.

I remember springtime, the beautiful children before the maggots get into their eyes, and the flowers and the green park, and the earthen walls around the medina, and the Atlas mountains from the rooftop, and the endless roar of humans hidden from sight in the narrow labyrinths, each person pursuing a private purpose—the wanderers from Michigan awaiting money from home and the pregnant girl to give birth in that alien bedlam, the rapture on the faces listening to storytellers, the merchants hustling their wares or lounging back not giving a damn while you take your own time finding the right fit, the café owners smoking and drinking tea, the boy with a letter from a Californian girl and dreams of America, the stranger passing through on his way to New York who couldn't talk English or even French but couldn't go home or he'd by shot by his government. Those days were like a secret door that I passed through freely.

Meanwhile it's cold here and I'm alone, and the walls are quiet but the sky has a gash like an open wound and disease festers wherever warmth is trapped.

Wanderlust

It is above sixty-five and the sun is shining and people are walking around on the sidewalks smiling or sitting in front of their houses and stores and digging it!

K is leaving in a few days. He's on top of the world, packing and selling books and giving them away, hot to trot.

I've been working on the railroad, and soon I'll have a couple grand and be off for the south, with Rio the final goal,

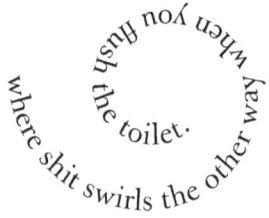
where shit swirls the other way when you flush the toilet.

The cold winter
introversion tells me
I should stay and learn a trade
        but the sunshine says
           go! life is warmer outside
        the institutions.
               It is pleasanter to be
               a soldier of fortune
               than a fortunate soldier
                     in *any* army.

Wanderlust

Life on the
        railroad stays
                on the same tracks
and the same trains
        run at the same
                time each night.

It's all the same, all the same, all the same, all the same, all the same, all the same, all the same, all the same, all the same, all the sa

Come the cruelest month, I'll visit the hard rock of Montana and the green liquid hills of Seattle and the concrete flowerpots of California and the gun-toting rednecks of Montrose and the twisted sameness of Friday night barrooms in Durango and hot moist francophone Louisiana, wending ever southward toward the water, the Gulf, until I finally fall

off

the

edge

to the other side of the world.

Scars

What's life worth if in its living we don't pick up some scars?

I cherish the scar on my nose from the train wreck, the scar on my head from the Sioux who tried to scalp me, the scar on my chest from the samurai hoodlum who narrowly missed the center of my life's blood, the one on my eardrum from my descent into the Hellhole off Bermuda, that unhealable one left on my heart by the strange and beautiful princess of Tibet, the gash on my foot caused by—I don't think you knew of this episode in my otherwise dull and uneventful existence—a shattered crystal goblet let slip by the emperor of the Celestial Realm (this on my return, sadder but wiser, from Tibet), the pain of which I strove to ignore as I rushed to his side—the expiring end of a long and glorious dynasty—becoming aware of myself again only after he had passed in my arms from this sphere into that other, greater paradise beyond us poor mortals, having confided to me, his one true and—if I may be so bold—trusted companion a grave secret relating to a theretofore unsuspected side of the imperial will, only then noticing the blood gushing from my severed vein to soil the hallowed floor as members of his retinue rushed into the chamber and took the lifeless body from my arms. I was forced to flee that night. Rumor had come that rivals jealous of my influence on the deceased emperor approached with intent that I should never again see great Aurora spread her rosy fingertips in the east. The flight I will not describe. It follows the pattern of all nocturnal emissions: The emperor's beautiful concubine, my trusty munji servant, the frail boat and muffled oars, fear of discovery by day and stealthy advance by night, lamentable loss of craft and companions to the torrent only yards before the rapids were passed, treachery of an embassy guard, and finally my clandestine arrival in Singapore to search the dingy alleys for the man whose name had been whispered in my ear by the dying monarch.

But I have digressed.

The Dentimale

Pursuing thence my travel across tractless Bifurkhistan, I happened upon an aboriginal tribe yclept the Dentimale, that is, "of the rotten teeth," known locally as Urtęr, which appellation derived from the Indo-Sanskrit roots for "urine" and "earth" signifies "brown-piss." This epithet is based upon a peculiar event which I shall now relate.

    Tradition has it that a short stranger with brown hair and eyes, no scars or other distinguishing marks and dressed only in a tweed overcoat, arrived from the north and proceeded through the country unto the great temple of Bhtą in the city of Lllł where, throwing the flaps of his garment aside, he relieved himself against the side of the holy edifice whilst uttering the incantation "Pssnnnit." Then, revealing himself to a multitude of outraged worshippers, he declaimed loudly, "Pssnnllłffu." In the ensuing general perplexity, he buttoned up his coat and made his way out of the country. It appears that he left by the southern border, but I have been unable to verify this.

THE ASKIYAN REVOLUTION

I bolted my café au lait in one gulp, which brought a lump to my throat and tears to my eyes, and fell choking to the ground at the feet of a blind lottery ticket seller, who tumbled with a beauty I had never seen—arms and legs aflail, cane somersaulting gracefully through the air, dozens of resplendent lottery tickets fluttering to the ground. His chin struck my knee causing no end of pain, and he lay unconscious atop me. I discreetly pushed him under a table and, figuring when in a foreign country speak a foreign language, muttered "Shquar a la bei" to the astonished onlookers and slunk limping down the street.

(*Shquar a la bei* is a medieval Songhai revolutionary slogan which means *Sack the sail,* a reference to the king's sailboat. King Sonni Bāru kept a sailboat in the landlocked city of Tumbutu. The boat was mounted on four wheels and every Sunday three thousand slaves ran behind and blew into the sail to propel the king around his estate. Although the revolution was precipitated by light-headed thinking caused by hyperventilation, its roots were deeper. To consolidate his power after the death of his father, the king had confiscated all the sacks in the country because they were being used for smuggling daggers to the slaves. He revealed to the court his plan to sew the sacks into a sail and the campaign became known by the slogan *Bei la'a shquar,* or *Sail the sacks,* which caused titters among the ladies (Johnson & Fitch, 1942).

The revolutionary leader Muhammad Ture two years later took as his slogan *Shquar a la bei.* He promised to remove this burden from the enslaved populace, and indeed upon his accession to power the sail was cut up and remade into sacks. Alas, they were now worthless for smuggling daggers. More than two million slaves had spat into the sail to show their contempt. (The king thought it was ocean spray.) The cloth was impregnated with moisture and rusted any metal it touched. Ture consequently oppressed in his turn the peons who had brought him to power, since they were unable to obtain replacement arms for the ones they had beaten into plowshares. (The episode of Muhammad Ture and his flying carpet held aloft by slaves accounts for *Shquar a la bei* coming to signify the sad recognition that revolutions serve only to exchange one tyranny for another. (Johnson & Fitch, 1944, *inter alios*)))

In the Royal Tombs of Ur

A rectangular shaft sloped ten meters down to the two rooms of the tomb. Walls were of rough limestone faced with mud plaster or cement and roofs were vaulted or domed. The inner chamber was for the principal body and the outer for victims of lesser standing. Bodies, in a coffin or not, were laid on reed mats and decked with finery, semiprecious stones (carnelian, lapis lazuli), silver, gold, and bronze. Vessels of copper, clay, silver, gold or stone held food and drink. Attendants crouched nearby. Sacrifice was a prerogative of godhead, and in fact later Sumerian kings were deified. Since gods don't die, death was merely translation to another sphere.

The doorway was blocked with clay brick and stone and plastered smoothly over. The first part of the ceremony was complete.

Into the open pit outside the tomb came a procession of members of the court, soldiers, manservants, women in brightly colored fabric and delicate headdresses. Then musicians with harps, lyres, cymbals and systra. Then chariots drawn by asses or oxen, the drivers in the cars and grooms walking beside. Each man and woman carried a small cup of clay, stone or metal. Potion was prepared in a copper pot at the bottom. Since hashish and opium were local products, perhaps the potion contained them. A rite took place, all composed themselves and dipped their cups. The musicians played to the last. Someone came down to kill the animals and arrange any drugged bodies that had become disarranged.

Different ranks and functions formed a household of sacrificial victims: Two or three personal servants, grooms, drivers, musicians, ladies of the harem, military officers, the keeper of the queen's wardrobe, soldiers on guard at the door–the court that had attended the king during life. The translation of a king caused a significant turnover in the ruling class.

The principal was provided with the necessary furniture of the dead and retained his personality but his subordinates did not. They were his chattels like the cups, spears, oxen and harps; it was not their funeral and they did not require the provisions which were his right. They were not even placed in the attitude in which the dead were laid.

Earth was flung from above into the pit to a certain height and a floor of trodden clay laid. More rites: Drink offerings were poured, fires lit, and on a small piece of matting (the original table of the nomad) a feast–the "table of god"–was prepared with small cups and plates, drink and bakemeats, and over them a great inverted clay bowl to keep them undefiled by earth.

The filling of the shaft continued until another pause for smoothing the surface and plastering with clay. The space was filled with a layer of earth, a layer of clay, another of earth, another of clay, and on each clay floor were offerings: vessels of food, animal bones, a human victim.

The final floor was prepared and crowded with gifts from the highest and the humblest: gold daggers, the king's signet, hundreds of clay saucers, the paraphernalia of death. The chamber was roofed with mats spread over rafters and daubed with clay. More earth was thrown in until the shaft was full. A chapel built above later served as a guide for grave robbers.

The ritual took weeks and months.

Simple graves were merely holes in the ground with much luxury but no other victims. And a good thing that was for the perpetuation of the race.

It is sad to visit the Sumerian collection at the Louvre, sad to read the fragments of text found by chance, the broken remains of a literature and society which was complete and self-referent, bits of sentences, incomplete thoughts, prayers, curses and transactions mounted with care and preserved under glass, glimpses of a spark or two from the sunlight of days past when other men and women led their daily lives and wrote a thought which sat on a shelf and as the years passed was transported and forgotten. Raiders came or drought and the people left, and the house slowly crumbled over the centuries and wind came with dust, and floods came, and rats and birds, and the earth covered it all and the sun beat down. And here it is now.

IN THE ROYAL TOMBS OF EGYPT'S OLD KINGDOM

Fake doors became operable after death, and to the extent that things in life were useless they became efficacious.

The Cappadocian Cave Network

The recent discovery of a vast cave network in Anatolia has caused great excitement among not only troglodytes but anthropologists.

Négresse Station (Biarritz)

Followed by What's-Her-Name I sauntered into the station to take the next train to San Sebastian. We'd been hitchhiking since morning into the misty seaside dusk and early evening, and were tired of standing for hours on end with our thumbs out.

There was a crowd of Frenchmen standing around the ticket counter but nobody was behind it. At that very instant a train pulled into the station, breathing steam and hissing like Fafnir. Seeing no need to buy a ticket from a nonexistent clerk, I proposed to WHN that we board without one. She was all for observing established custom and waiting until a clerk showed up, even if that was after the dragon left. I was forced to drag her protesting body onto the quay and push her into a car.

The train left at once. We slunk down the corridor searching for an empty compartment. There were few passengers and practically all the seats were free. I led until my intuition signaled the correct compartment, which by dint of grunts and hand signals I persuaded WHN was the one destined for us.

The train swept through a dense countryside in silence broken only by the deafening screech of iron wheels upon iron rails. I expected a cloaked figure to rush into the compartment, leap through the window and disappear into the murk followed hotly by two or three gendarmes with drawn revolvers. Instead, a swarthy Arab appeared outside the window on a carpet which he offered to sell us below the going rate. I was a bit unsettled because my intuition had failed to foresee this. We threw an empty cigarette pack to him and he veered off, leaving us in peace.

Soon the train entered a long, well-lit station. I peered out the window and saw everyone getting off and walking some three or four hundred yards to enter the building by a small door. I told WHN to follow me. We descended and headed for a much closer door. She was of the opinion that we should go where the rest of the people were going, but I rejected this both on principle and because it was so far to walk.

Inside the door a customs agent looked at us with surprise. I instantly realized that we were entering by the door for people returning from Spain, but was loathe to exit and use the proper door because it would be discovered that we had no tickets. In France, if one is discovered without a ticket, he is incarcerated without trial. Knowing foreign customs as I do, having spent my life travelling in search of fleece, I knew this peculiarity and was determined not to be found out.

I walked straight up to the officer and asked, "Which way to San Sebastian?"

Struck speechless by the apparition of two travelers arriving in French customs from the French side of the border, he wrote directions on a scrap of paper. We were to leave by the door opposite, turn left, and walk a kilometer over the bridge into Spain. San Sebastian would then be only nineteen klicks away. I thanked him, glanced at the paper and memorized the instructions, then burned it so we would leave no trail. Once in Spain we would be safe.

We crossed the border, waving our passports at the guards. They smiled and asked for chocolate bars or chewing gum. I had not thought to come stocked with such gifts, but I pulled some buttons off WHN's blouse and proffered those. The guards bowed low and accepted with gestures of gratitude.

WHN no longer had any idea of where we were or what was happening, or even who we were. I refreshed her memory, and we began the long walk into Irun.

A dirty city it was, teeming with gentry out for their evening stroll. For a moment I thought we had crossed into Juarez, but got a grip on myself and charged on. We stopped to ask three nuns the way to the train station but didn't know the Spanish words, and they looked at us with apprehension and fear. That was not surprising, as my head was aglow and WHN's crotch was dripping incandescent sparks. Thinking to bring some excitement into the lives of these poor sisters of Christ, I raised my fingers in the gesture of the diabolic horns. They screamed, attracting the attention of two Guardia Civil strolling by. These gentlemen lowered their machine guns and assumed the ready stance. Thinking quickly, I reached over to WHN and ripped her pants down. The brilliance dazzled the soldiers and permitted our hasty escape, WHN stumbling a little as she tried to run with pants around her knees.

Luckily, we found the station just as a train was pulling in. We dashed down a long inclined plane to the ticket office. I pushed some of the strange Spanish money at the clerk and croaked, "Two for San Sebastian." He gave me two tickets and change, and we boarded the train which at that instant jerked and pulled out.

Noticing the eyes of all the men in car upon us, I whispered to WHN, "Pull up your pants." She did, but the men continued to stare. I saw nothing to do about it, so I suggested we ignore them.

WHN looked like she was in shock. I surmised that she was unused to the queer quality of international travel, having arrived from a small town in Kansas only two days before. In an attempt to startle her into her right mind, I leaned close and muttered the Holy Fool password into her ear, "Schquar a la bei." This had the unfortunate result of causing her to jump away and begin sobbing. I was nonplussed.

To add to my dismay, the train started and stopped at short intervals. I found myself losing the thread of my intuition and was not sure I would recognize the proper stop. I was torn between consoling WHN and reestablishing the link with my subconscious at the risk of losing her entirely. The biological imperative shouted, "Let the weak transmogrify!" but compassion won me over. I put my hand down her pants and rubbed gently until she relaxed.

The crisis passed. The train stopped. I glanced out the window and intuition poked me in the ribs. "Let's go," I said.

WHN clung to me as we got off the train and walked into the center of town. Her eyes were now entirely acquiescent. She no longer had thoughts of her own and was ready to heed my slightest suggestion. It was a bit disgusting. I have seen many people crack under the stress of travel but never to the extent that she had. I didn't know what to do with her. I knew I would be better off in the coming battle if I were unencumbered by her total lack of volition. In fact, I could already feel its effect on my awareness. Some of the buildings around us were slipping into a hazy fog and others had already disappeared. Yet I felt I was responsible for her condition, having imposed my will on hers until she arrived at her present state. The humane thing to do was keep her with me until I could ensure her recovery. It was a damned nuisance, though.

We marched through the streets looking for a hotel. I asked everyone we met if they knew of one but was unable to make myself understood. Nothing unusual in that, but I was getting tired and old WHN obviously could go little further. Luckily, a small man wearing a cap understood and beckoned us to follow.

He led us through the twisting streets into a narrow sinister door. Up the stairs we went, up and up, until I was sure we had reached the sky. I suspected him of luring us into this hellish niche only to abandon us, so I dogged his feet. A quick glance out a skylight reassured me that the sky was still above. Unless, of course, it was only a mockup. I refused to consider the possibility.

Finally our little cortege reached the top. The small man knocked on a door and a tremendously fat woman appeared. They conversed in a foreign tongue and then the woman smiled and showed us to a room furnished only with two beds and a nightstand. She indicated by means of gestures that she wanted our passports. I pretended we had none, but she was adamant and I ended by giving them to her. She and the small man had a moment of hilarity when they compared the names on the passports. I suspect they thought we were just some ordinary couple who had come to San Sebastian for a weekend of fun and love. I did not say otherwise.

 WHN took one bed and I the other. As the day's tension receded, I wanted very much to have sex. She did not. I believe they do not do such things in Kansas outside marriage. She proposed instead a quaint old custom she told me of called bundling, where a young man and woman lie together on a bed separated by a sheet or blanket.

 I thought it was silly, but still, nothing propinques like propinquity, so I moved to her bed. She cheered up. Her infantile pleasure at controlling a situation for the first time in days was charming, but control was the operative word—if she lost that pleasure she would float away again. It was disheartening and I was tired. Tomorrow would be a day best met refreshed, so I pecked her cheek and fell asleep.

Langon

Standing in the train station waiting for the train to move so I can cross the tracks, I watch steam hiss from the coupling between two cars and am aware that I'm realizing my dream. I'm alone in a foreign country with no expectations.

Lately I've been feeling uneasy about having no solid plans, though I'm getting by fine: food to eat, places to stay, and enough money for the theater now and then. Watching the steam, I'm satisfied.

I'm surprised at how slowly my life moves, the length of time between events, the silence between contact with people like blank sleep between dreams. I'm realizing my dream here in this train station, and I realize it in the narrow Bordeaux streets thronged with people and small shops, and on the café terraces reading newspapers with their different slants. In all these places I feel the slow continuing realization of being in Europe and out of my own country. Always the same simple realization through mere physical presence. It's so simple that I have to keep reminding myself that I have fulfilled my desires simply by being here and that I have no other expectations.

Life is simple. It consists of these uneventful moments, these paving stones, this same sky over the towns. The towns differ only superficially—in the skyline, the street layout—they all have streets and a skyline and the same sky overhead. The differences are in the hopes I attach to each, the possibility of new dreams and a new life.

The places are the same and I am the same, but still I approach each place with expectancy and acceptance. I come fresh to each empty loom as yarn to be woven into the people and the landscape.

So I watch the steam and know I'm doing all I should. In living this dream, as I am woven into this world, I will change and find new ways to follow.

Saint Macaire

When I graduated from college my draft deferment ended. I managed to drag out my physical for a year but figured they'd get me in the end, so I decided to move to France, where Chrétien D had arranged a job harvesting grapes for the family B. Just before I left I was mistakenly given a permanent deferment, and as I had planned to leave for good it was a relief knowing the bridge wouldn't burn behind me.

I'm staying in the family D's spare room, which gives onto the main truck route between somewhere and somewhere else, so all is not exactly peace and quiet. But it has beautiful old furniture, a marble fireplace that doesn't work, a huge bed whose flea-infested mattress resembles the small summit of a steep mountain, four large mirrors, and a table with a light where I have my typewriter and from which I gratefully survey my possessions: two guitars, harmonicas, a couple dictionaries and elementary physics books, sheet music, clothes, skis, and skin diving equipment. I'm equipped with all the luxuries I need save a hot shower.

I like best the little outhouse downstairs. This isn't like the modern one behind the house proper across the street, where water flushes the toilet bowl for as long as you depress the lever. To get to this one, you walk half a dozen paces under the sky between another building and a wall that must have been built four centuries ago. Inside you lift a small wooden cover and seat yourself over the hole cut into a bench of regal dimensions. Then you contemplate the surrounding walls, or if you leave the door open as is my wont, you gaze at the sky over the wall and roofs of the neighboring houses. The outhouse walls on your left and behind are stone; the other two are of wood. How many outhouses have walls of worked stone? Seated thus, I wonder how old the shit beneath me is. It may be no older than in other outhouses I've met, but I am conscious of a great difference in tradition. The shit in Colorado, say, is a product of the timeless sky, the mountains, and the crystal air, which never change though they vary with the hours and seasons; thus the shit lies in the eternal present. Here kingdoms rise and republics fall, different races pass through and each leaves its trace, the town grows like an animal, the air is tamed to human dimensions and painters borrow its softness for their canvas, and the shit changes with the different leavings from this flux, this human ebb and flow. I drop in my little bit where it is soon assimilated.

But alas, man does not live by bread and trips to the outhouse alone. There isn't much to do. Eat, sleep, play guitar, write (I tell people I'm writing stories but I can't finish any; I write letters mostly), fight the crab lice that have accompanied me from Colorado. The wine harvest starts next week and will last until the end of November. I impatiently await the start of manual labor. When your body is exhausted by a day of good solid exertion, your mind is calm. Also adding to my tranquility will be the knowledge that I'm making money to replace what I've been spending at a furious rate. And a job does give you the feeling that you're accomplishing something worthwhile, doesn't it? I have to keep telling myself that I'm perfecting my French, too. One curse of bourgeois education is the need to always feel that I'm accomplishing something.

Chrétien took me through the building he just bought, next door to the one with my room. Many nice things are there: old books, gloves from the 1890s with a device to stretch the fingers before you put them on, a light fixture counterbalanced on pulleys for raising and lowering, a bed warmer, some very old saws, pictures of his father as a child, a beautiful porcelain wash basin with a reservoir above that you fill with hot water. Open the faucet at the base and the water runs over your hands into the basin. He discovered that the garage belonged to his mother's grandfather. The name is stamped on one of the walls, and another wall is that of some 14th century monument. He's going to dig through the archives and talk to the old people to find out exactly what it was.

Where did they come from, these filthy little beasts? Nits apparently dead but obviously containing the potential for life must have stuck to hairs all over my body as we flew through the lifeless sky six miles above the ocean where life began. The kerosene I had used to kill them came from the same epoch as their ancestors; no doubt they were ancient acquaintances. Although the fossil drink was too strong for the lice kinetic, their potential phase had learned to slumber during all the millions of years their vegetable sisters were brewing, their own forms of life crushed into mineral. The eggs remained organic and untouched by the kerosene. Old friends, they were. Then the buggers leaped out of the past to crawl over my body.

Chrétien took me into a pharmacy and I marched to the counter and would have said, "Do you have something for crabs?" but Chrétien restrained me and said, "This young American is afflicted with body parasites... Could you assist...?" We left with a small bottle of blue mercury-based ointment.

The harvest began and I was completely exhausted and sore for the first three days. Now I'm just exhausted. It's backbreaking—stooping or squatting and clipping and placing the warm plump bunches of grapes into a bucket and taking it full to a 250 liter barrel at the end of the row—but the soreness faded and it is lovely under the clear blue sky overlooking a valley of golden vineyards with easy banter among the other three youths in the crew—Monsieur B's son Joël, and Maurice and Jackie from the village. Some days another young man, Jean-Marie, joins us.

Monsieur B is a small old man proud to be a peasant. He

recounts the neighborhood goings on, life under the Germans during the war, and droll examples of human nature. He explains how the world price of gold fluctuates, why Italy entered the war, why he has a Russian crescent wrench and an American tractor.

He knew a man who avoided work for twenty years by saying he had a heart condition. He lived with his brother and got unemployment compensation when he could. One day the brother said Enough! Get a job! Protestations, arguments. Finally the man got a job and died two days later.

Before the first world war a man kept a café and hotel in Langon across from the train station. Clients disappeared. He was killing them and dumping the bodies in the river, but was finally caught.

It turns out that the family B is quite accepting of my motives, as Monsieur B himself ran away from the Pétain government draft.

We work from 8 to 12 and 2 to 6, and this is the only place I've been where you drink on the job. Every hour or so we break for a couple minutes and have a glass of wine. I've been mildly to extremely intoxicated for four days. If my kidneys don't disintegrate, I'll learn yet how to drink.

My sister is in Bordeaux for her junior year abroad, three years after I was there for mine. I accompanied her group on an outing to Arcachon and must say things are going well for me. I find I have a lot of prestige, having been here before and knowing my way around. Half a dozen girls are interested in me, and thanks to my sister I know which ones. I chose the prettiest to saunter around with, eat oysters, drink wine, the things a young couple does in a French seashore resort town. I had to return to St Macaire that night but we're off to San Sebastian this weekend.

The director of my sister's program is impassioned by Proust. He's editor of a Proust monthly, has edited his notes for publication and is writing two books about him, so I bought *A la recherche du temps perdu* to have something to talk about. It'll be interesting to compare Proust's representation of time with Bergson, Nabokov and Durrell, though I can't say I quite grasp any of them totally, but my misunderstanding gives rise to my own ideas.

At the moment I'm terribly worried about money, although there is no reason to be. I'm alive and well, and have 224.74 francs, 1400 pesetas, and 1 dollar. Got the dollar in the mail today. Plus 60 dollars in travelers checks, and I sold my metal-stringed guitar for 546.25 francs which I haven't received yet. My pay is 200 francs (40 dollars) and two bottles of red a week or another 10 francs if I don't want the wine. Well, I ought to be able to eat on weekends for a while.

My fellow harvesters drink water during breaks but force wine on me, so I'm tipsy when I join Chrétien's family for lunch. Wine there. Back to the vineyard and more vinous breaks. At five we load the barrels on the wagon and the tractor pulls it to the shed where we dump them into a concrete vat and drink an aperitif relaxing and chatting and watching the river flow. Walk to Chrétien's and dinner with wine and a pousse-café and then to bed.

Weekends when I visit my sister I take my two bottles and flirt with the girls. After a stretch of mild intoxication for a week and weekend and following week, I insisted on water during the breaks. Monsieur B wouldn't hear of it.

"But you're all drinking water," I said.

"But you're the American guest," he said.

I was loathe to decline his kindness and hospitality but stood my ground.

Joel and Maurice speak a weird form of French, lots of slang and many Languedoc words, one of the languages descended from Latin. It's still spoken exclusively by some of the older people. After working with them for the day and not quite understanding everything they say, the language spoken around the Ds' dinner table is a breeze. I'm even able finally to do some joking. In a couple months I will be fluent. Especially living like this, where the only English I see is in letters from home and what I write. (Not counting weekends in Bordeaux.) I'm dreaming in French. The most frustrating times are when I nick myself with the scissors used to cut the bunches from the vine, or slam my thumb in a door, or something like that. The reaction is immediate but halfway through saying something like Ow goddammit, I realize it's English, and by the time I find the correct French obscenity, it's too late. Alone in my bedroom at night I practice slamming my hand in a drawer and swearing.

I'm learning words in another language, too. Occitane, another Latin language, is still spoken by the older people. There is a movement underway to revive the culture and language of Occitania, the region in the south of what is now France. There is a similar sentiment in northern Spain where Catalan was the language of the modern Castilians. I'm becoming an Occitanian nationalist. Fight the constipation of the Anglo-Saxon-Celtic northerners!

Some evenings, the harvest crew excavates a twelfth century priory which an army from Bordeaux destroyed three or four hundred years ago. It's a pleasure to join them and pass buckets of dirt up the ladder. They tell me that now I'm an official member of the Midi.

This week I have the vocabulary of a five-year-old. By the middle of February, I might have the vocabulary of a twenty-one-year-old, but I'll be twenty-two. Come one, come all, see the great race between Achilles and the tortoise.

I want to be able to speak this language fluently and need practice, but sometimes it is so much trouble to express even a simple thought that I only sketch it, let someone else fill it in, and then agree with what they say. It must be wearing for them to guess my meaning and say it for me. Sometimes I say to myself what the hell and struggle to get it out, poor as it may sound. I think my silences are rude so I strike up conversation with everyone I meet but I'm also shy so I mainly ask questions and let them do the talking.

I don't talk much with the Ds, though, because nobody in that family likes anyone else. All they do is quarrel and complain, and since there are seven of them, there's a lot of quarreling. I keep my mouth shut. They all treat me kindly, though. I wonder how I must appear to them, silent as a stick. Thank god, thank the lord in heaven, there's a job in the grape fields that keeps me out of the house.

I've been feeling at loose ends. The curé told me not to worry about having no plans. God will give me faith. If one searches during life, God takes him to heaven afterwards and helps him continue the search—heaven is continuation of perfection. Interesting thought, that heaven is a process, not a static condition.

All people feel the desire to travel, he said, which he interprets as the desire to escape. Films, particularly westerns, are a means of escape. When one is young, life seems to go by very slowly, but as one grows older, gets married and has a situation, it goes by faster. He remembers the occupation as if it were yesterday. Then he warned me against spending my life roaming around not doing anything, being always on holiday, and he warned me against pride, individualism, and the cult of self-sufficiency. Well, his job is admonishing people. He certainly has a proselytizing manner, as do they all, these priests. They're more interested in people as converts to their way of thinking than as the individuals they are. I did agree that man needs something greater than his personal preoccupations, but according to him God is that which is greater for which we search. He professes respect for the Carthusian monks who contemplate God individually and avoid seeing other people. There, he says, is a vocation given by God.

An amiable man very forward with his opinions. He distrusts the Germans and thinks the Russians keep Germany divided because they don't trust them either, and says the genius of France is that of rejecting ideas: they don't get carried away by any idea for too long. Told me the Bs are anticlerical, too political, radical in fact, almost communists, and said he would he'd set me up with some *good* people for next year's harvest.

Chrétien's reaction: "The bastard!"

My fellow harvesters were disgusted. "He's a hypocrite! He's against the excavation of the priory but he shows it off to visitors. What bullshit!"

Regarding aimless travel, everyone wants to. Antoine the antique dealer would like to but is held down by his family and job. He hopes his son will be a journalist and get to travel.

M le curé could have gone to French Guiana for a marriage but wouldn't leave his old mother alone.

Chrétien would like to live in the US but can't because of having a family.

Lou and Greg wanted a tranquil life so they moved to Placerville and when they tired of that they moved to San Francisco. Good for them, and me, too, for coming here.

I took a walk and a good book to the old part of town. Narrow, high streets, carvings in the stone walls, dates (1879, 1646). Monsieur B showed me a parcel of land that was sold to his forebears by Chrétien's forebears a couple hundred years ago. The present is alive with the past here.

Let yourself sink, Jack, sink without struggle, for it only impedes the descent and breaks the glide. Let yourself fall, empty your lungs of air, spread your arms and swan downward. Try a flip or two, gracefully. No panic. Don't hinder the beauty; you're going down struggle or not, and you'll enjoy it more if you relax. When you drown, sink all the way.

The sooner you hit bottom, the sooner you will rise. After a while the spectacle of your misery will grow too much to take seriously. Indulge it until you see yourself as a writhing little worm, a self-indulgent baby among the grownups, and laugh at yourself. You'll say shit, man, have a look—haven't you had enough? Are you as weak as this? To twist and bawl in your insomnia?

So sink, Jack. Go home and have a good cry. Feel deep down how miserable you are. You've lost another lover, you can't write a dad-blamed thing, you're alone with no goal in life, you can't speak the language, your far-off friends are all happy in their homes... It gets hard to keep a straight face, but wait, don't laugh yet. Remember that even if you could talk French the Ds don't want to hear what you have to say, you eat too much at meals, you go back to your cold dark room and can't play your guitar, you aren't interested in books, you are bored utterly, you're doing nothing, just living through the day until you can sleep and then get up again to this emptiness. (When you do nothing, you do it alone. I want to spend my life in something that involves people—theater, music, skiing, medicine, teaching.)

You haven't hit bottom yet. You can go further. Go until people don't want you around anymore because you sit and mope. When you run out of things to feel bad about, invent some. Suppose the Ds want you to leave and you're stuck in St Macaire with no job and no money so you borrow from your parents and return home. What would you find there? The same sense of aimlessness and lack of accomplishment, plus dismay at a wasted trip to Europe.

I wanted to come here. I came. I'm here. I still want to go to Greece and the Far East. I'll wait for this winter's plans to gel. If I don't get a job, I can go to the Canaries by way of Morocco and apply for a job where Jon works. Or maybe find a boat to Guiana to see Michel and then head back to the US.

I've been accepted for training as a ski instructor at Val d'Isère but have decided to become a doctor, and I've begun by trying to kill the third incarnation of these damn body lice. First kerosene, then mercury, now DDT. We'll probably all die together.

It's back to Denver where I can talk to deans of admission, send letters without a two-week delay, get a job, and do the necessary to start med school next fall.

I'm sad my voyages are almost over for a good number of years, but I'm content. I want to start now, can't wait. I will get foreign jobs later.

Bordeaux to Denver

Caught the 9:05 bus from Place de la Victoire to Gradignan to start hitchhiking.

After 10 minutes, a ride that took me 6 kilometers out of Bordeaux.

After 10 minutes, a young physical therapist who works with cripples took me to 12 kilometers north of Bayonne. Flat tire along the way.

After 3 minutes, a man from Grenoble who chuckled at Denver's refusing the Olympics. Grenoble is still paying for theirs, he said, but at least they got new highways, stadiums, and so forth. If Denver is really out, Grenoble will bid for 1976 which would pay off their debts completely. He chuckled a lot at that.

He told me of the custom of the *cerraros* in Madrid, *les serreurs,* to whom everyone on the block gives the keys to their houses. The serreur locks up at 22:00 and anyone who needs in after that stands in the street and claps. He hears, comes, and lets them in.

After a nice walk along the coast highway from St Jean de Luz, a ride to San Sebastian. The driver asked hesitantly, "Est-ce que vous êtes français?" "Je suis américain." "Ah, je me disais... un petit accent." Gratifying.

Reached San Sebastian at 15:00. Lousy meal in town and then the train to Madrid at 16:17.

A Hungarian Rhapsody of Lizst on the express. Jet plane snack of Pepsi and cold cuts served on slip-in trays. Everyone talking Spanish.

What a smile on the face of the two-year-old walking in

the aisle. What a smile of kinship and recognition between her and the eight- and ten-year-olds next to me. They smile at my difficulty writing, the difficulty of drinking without spilling, the length of a tunnel.

Me with hemorrhoids (pain walking, standing, sitting) and completely lost in the new language and customs. For example, I got on the higher priced train (961 pts) rather than the cheaper. But with food! Served! My god. And to think that I thought I would have so much trouble getting around. And faster. I'll arrive at 22:30 instead of 9:00 tomorrow.

The little Spanish boy watched me write. I said to him, Es ingles, and then wrote in French to blow his mind. I immediately felt like a jerk, but it kept coming until the end of the sentence. Then I quit. What a dirty trick.

Arrived in Madrid and walked across town to be near the Prado and the other train station. Some jerk from the US military base accosted me, gave me American cigarettes, talked about re-upping, his girl, how cheap life is here, and rushed off to catch his bus back to the base.

I walked around looking for a pension or a cheap hotel. All I found were expensive hotels and dark pensiones. Then I saw a couple applauding in the middle of the street and remembered the serreurs so I walked around the corner and started clapping. A little old man appeared. I said pension, he said no and lot of other things and pointed. I said gracias and went that way and clapped again. Another old man appeared and led me to a pension. The lady said 80, I understood 800, was dismayed at the high price and then embarrassed at my mistake but not for long as she was used to this and I was dead tired and my piles hurt. In bed at 0:30 and slept until 11:30.

Consigned my things at the train station, had coffee, went to the Prado. Breughel did a good one called *Triumph of Death,* much like Bosch (El Bosco). Looked at Goya and Rubens, my piles were killing me, scanned Greco.

Bosco means woods. Greco means Greek. Flamenco means Flemish.

Walked around the old part of town, saw the flea market, people-to-people streets, one street selling nothing but caged birds, feed, cages, calcium. Everything was outside.

Decided I wouldn't be needing a cholera booster shot because I wasn't going anywhere it was active.

20:10 train. Slept in cot at top of compartment. Fourteen hours in the train. Found I could make simple sentences in Spanish but was too shy to say much.

10:30 Algeciras. I'd been there before, knew where to go, what to do. Changed money, bought ticket, wasted no time. 12:00 boat to Tanger, the same old boat, the *Ibn Batuta,* same old dolphins in the water. Arrived at 14:30 thanks to picking up an hour in time change. I was disgusted with the hustle that began on the gangplank, but I knew the score and where I was going, so I ignored it and thought, fuck it, if a price is reasonable, I won't haggle.

Morocco, the tower of Babel. The first thing anyone asks is what language you speak. They almost always sized me up and asked if I spoke English. I replied in French, talked in French. When in a foreign country, speak a foreign language. Later, in the Canaries, I decided that you just speak whatever people understand, but in Morocco it irked me to be typed as American and treated like a rich hippy tourist.

The boy who led me to the public bath I used three years before amazed me by the assured air with which he asked ten dirhams. I think my jaw actually dropped. Not that I wasn't expecting something outrageous—it was the cool way he put it. I gave him 3.50, still outrageous, no doubt.

15:30 train to Casablanca, second class, 31 dirhams, cars like cabooses with varnished wood exteriors, very good seats, two rows of two facing forward in each compartment, but terrific noise. The shriek from the wheels on the tracks was so loud in the WC that I shouted full out without hearing myself, only feeling the muscles tense. The third class trains looked like cattle trains.

From Tanger through Asilah, Ksar el-Kebir, Sidi Slimane, Kenitra, Rabat to Casablanca at 21:30 with 40 dollars, 80 French francs, and 60 dirhams. Slept in the medina—ugly, hustling, scary.

ITO Atwater, the American Express branch in Casablanca, said there were no boats to the Canaries, so I walked to the docks and asked around about freighters. There would be none until at least next week. I changed money at the bank, bought a plane ticket for the biweekly flight to Las Palmas for 212 dirhams, and telegraphed Jon telling him when I would arrive. I figured it would be more expensive and less enjoyable to stay three days in Casablanca than somewhere else, so I bought a bus ticket for 4.80 d to El Jadida because it was not far and on the coast. The bus took two hours to go the 80 kilometers. Found a hotel, walked around and met a young man named Abdullah.

Abdullah told me about the blue men of the Sahara with skin blackened by the sun who dress in blue and ride camels. They are magicians. There are strong magicians in the south, old wizened men, not like the phonies in Casablanca or Tanger or even El Jadida. Give one 5 dirhams and somebody's full name; he will describe their features. (Abdullah pointed out a blind lady the next day in the souk who could do this.) He can describe the looks of the girl you will marry and he can make spells to render a girl amorous.

During holy month the girls save the cloth they use to clean their genitals. On the 27th day they put it in a jar of acid, and as it dissolves it tears the heart of the man they want, rendering him desirous of her. She must act quickly though, for the spell wears off fast and revulsion sets in—he swears at her and beats her.

People the age of his grandparents told Abdullah that if a person walks the streets alone in the dark night and steps in chicken's blood, he will see the devil approach as a dark form and will be possessed. Symptoms include acting crazy, epilepsy, spastic movement. This is cured by putting keys in the possessed's right hand and a pitchy tar that smells like waterproofing grease for boots in his nostrils. (I saw an old man in the souk selling this.) The demon departs at once.

Then there are men who dedicate their lives to Allah, true slaves of God who fast and pray. Some are snake-charmers. When they die a temple is erected in their honor and people leave gifts of money, food, candles, jewelry, so that the holy man will intercede for them with God. Women, mostly, leave the gifts, barren women, for example, and attach strings and threads to the temple doorknocker for luck. Beggars stay by the door to hit them up.

The present secretary of the PTT is a former general who had been given three or four battalions by the French. He went to the desert to fight and returned alone after a week. They accused him of selling his soldiers. He asked for another battalion and was given one (who was foolish enough to do that? or corrupt?) but again returned alone. Accused again of slave-trading, he replied that he had been fighting but all his men were killed. To show how he had survived, he asked them to shoot him from six meters. They did; he was unharmed. Later his brother let it be known that only a silver bullet would kill him.

The king fears a short man who controls the Rif mountains and wants to control the rest of the South, too. (The PTT minister?) Someone who lives in the hills, the Rif. Someone was killed.

Abdullah has much respect for the men of the south and the Sahara, especially the blue men and the sorcerers.

He took me to a shop in the souk where I bought a rhaita (a double reed instrument) and told me the strings attached near its mouthpiece are for luck like those on a temple door.

Evening in the back streets of El Jadida knocking cautiously on brothel doors, muttering in the omnipresent language of flous (fric, pognon, cash), veiled and djellabaed ladies, you don't know what you're getting into, following Abdullah into the tiled inner court of a hand-me-down Portuguese brothel (El Jadida was controlled by the Portuguese from 1502 to 1769), peeking into bedrooms at the girls, piss in the hole in the WC floor and go up the twisting staircase, sit stiffly on reclining couches that line the walls and wonder how you can fuck on such a narrow surface, maybe they put cushions on the floor and you slide around like dogs, never do find out because the madam comes and says she can't understand why none of the girls are here tonight, translated into poor mumbling French by A, waiting, everywhere waiting, for the train, the food, the passport control, for someone to show up, you forget what you're waiting for. A asks if I'm going to stay, he's leaving, we can leave the madam five dirhams so she knows we're really going to come back tomorrow and have some girls for us, we'll return with wine, olives, bread, cheese, pick our girls from the naked bevy, find me one that talks French and knows how to make love to a European. The girl in the room with us tells A I don't look like a European, my hair is short, I wonder what I look like then, certainly not an African, but she's probably just being nice, I don't have anything to say, thank you, just waiting. A and I get up to leave and he says give the lady some money, no more than five dirhams, okay, it's for tomorrow, I can knock five dirhams off the price tomorrow. Back in the street, the sinister twisting night streets of the old city, by myself I'd be quite unnerved but with A I'm a blithe spirit though he seems a bit edgy, probably knows more than I do about lurking murderers. I don't care.

Abdullah points out that dinner was extraordinarily cheap, 5 d for a fish dinner, sounds cheap to me, but he insists, 5 d for 8 fish, yeah but there were only 6–3 for me, 3 for him, 2 of which were "supplements" since he is a friend of the proprietor—I paid for two dinners and if I went back and got one 3-fish dinner it would still cost 5 d; plus 1d50 for a bottle of Vichy water which he says the proprietor had to go out and buy specially, but sometime earlier he said Eau de Vichy runs 0d50, so I paid 1 d for someone to get it, besides, I ordered lemonade, not Eau de Vichy, but it's okay, I got tales of sorcerers and werewolves with dinner, it was worth the price of Abdullah's meal, the whole thing probably would have cost a local 2d50 but what the heck.

Abdullah goes to great lengths to convince me I got a good deal and I don't even care. That's what gets to be a real drag fast in Morocco, money money everywhere, they steal it openly or take their cut in the corner while you aren't looking, hustle tourists all day and get one meal and 20 cents and it's been a good day. If they knew how much I don't care and were assured that they'd get theirs in the end would they relax?

I can accept it all and not get upset because I know I have a way out.

Youssef came up while I was on the jetty playing my rhaita and invited me to his house. I was tired of being hustled at every step, tired of everyone's childlike inquisitiveness, everyone wanting to look at the rhaita, asking questions, wanting my money and my time. I suppose they have so little that when someone gets something new or someone new shows up, they gather round to escape the monotony of their own lives. But Youssef didn't seem to be hustling.

My deep sadness at the poverty of mind and body at his home. The hole in the floor of his room where he pees. His one jacket, two shirts, one pair of shoes. His books: Malraux's *L'Espoir,* La Bruyère's *Pensées,* a pamphlet in French on modern Dutch painters, an advertising brochure in English for Mobil Oil. On the wall pictures of Hassan II, Raquel Welch, the "vrai visage de Jésu Christ" (a bloody bearded face), two film posters (westerns).

Pieces of pigeon in the plate of vegetables, with bread soaked in the sauce to help fill the stomach. I was very hungry but didn't want to eat all he had.

He served mint tea, and soon his sister-in-law came to take back the service because she needed it for another guest.

His papers: military discharge, carte d'identité (first and second), life saving certification, thesis from grade school, childhood drawings, permission to take a test to become a lifeguard next summer.

Designs he had done with colored inks on white silk. Very pretty, like Peter Max. He was out of silk and hoping that a friend in France would send him some.

All his letters and photos in a box. A couple pictures of naked women.

Correspondence with a girl from California he had met two year earlier. Her last letter was dated nine months ago. She had asked him to send her a djellaba, and asked how much money to send. He replied, asking what size to buy. She hadn't written back. He was upset.

I suggested that he write and tell her that perhaps her reply had been lost in the mail. He said he couldn't; it was her turn to write. I repeated the possibility that the letter had been lost. He repeated that it was her turn. I tried again and maybe he did understand, but was not convinced that he should write.

He thought she had simply abandoned him. I thought so too but didn't say so. I didn't want to hurt him. From the letter he let me read and the picture he had of her, it seems likely that he'd been a vacation fling.

I promised to write to her.

I promised to write to him.

I was very glad that the next day I would fly to Gran Canaria and Jon, books, ideas, wide-ranging knowledge, roughly same interests as mine, same culture and background.

Youssef found some friends with a guitar and we spent the evening in his room passing it around. A lousy guitar, but one of the kids played fantastic blues.

Gran Canaria

Jon was a college friend who now works at the manned space flight tracking center tucked away on the unseen side of a hill. His apartment is the second floor of a general store in El Tablero, with walls of white plaster and a white tile floor warm to the foot. A stair leads to the roof from where one can peer down to the dusty streets of the village or up to the dry peaks of the mountain that is the island, or turning around follow the planes of descending hills to the palm trees and glitter of the resort town on the beach.

The apartment's water piping must make up part of the electrical system. From sundown to midnight, when the village's diesel generator is running, you have to be careful not to ground yourself while washing your hands. Current passes easily through small cuts, I discovered—not pleasant, but better than the jolt when you grab the soap. I finally got caught in the shower when the power came on: blue spark, loud crack, and a strong shock to my forearm. I sprang out, pissed off that I wouldn't be able to shower until the next morning. Other people Jon knew had their own stories about local construction, like the toilet plumbed to the hot water.

Jon talks very much. To tell a story or even answer a simple question, he glosses and explicates until the whole thing is a series of parentheses. Now and again he stumbles across the thread of his speech, gives a theatrical start, and apologizes for wandering; but really he thinks his digressions are cute and reveal the workings of an over-fertile mind. He apologizes to make sure I notice.

We became friends because we had big egos. We sat around and talked philosophy and poetry and women and told each other how good we were. My ego is waning but his is still strong. Everything he says aims to be a brilliant insight that will provoke amazement and approval. I just wish he'd say what's on his mind and be done.

He says he prefers to live inside but actually he's afraid of the outside. I'm not surprised he knows few people—what energetic person would care to associate with him? He is horribly boring, like a newspaper listing the minutiae of the vomit which you skim with half an eye looking for real stuff (what actually happened) or the point of some pompous and irrelevant editorial. I have stopped listening to his sarcastic comments on the Canario character, his tedious and pretentious exaggerations of small incidents, his patronizing attitude toward the people who dance each Sunday, who play guitar and mandolin and accordion and sing and shout in the bars in the evenings—they have no desire, he says, to learn. (Maybe I would find them boring too, but first I would sing and shout and play guitar with them.) I've begun picking at him for ignoring what goes on around him. What irritates me is that he seems to do it willfully. But I'm being idiotic; he won't see what I'm driving at, and there's no point in getting upset.

As if his learning has helped him enjoy life any more than the untutored! It's turned him into a calculating machine who weighs histories and cultures and philosophies, and a poor one at that—he doesn't see the reasons for people's simplest actions. What does he hope to do with all his disputation? He says he wants to raise the consciousness of humanity. He'll have a hard time of it because when people suspect you think you're better than they are, they won't listen. I think he plans to invent a new philosophy that dazzles the philosophers. Fat chance.

He gripes about the drivers. (But he drives no less carelessly.) He gripes about the potholes in the roads. Well, once noticed and remarked upon, why not ignore them? I'm sure I too would soon know the route to work by heart, but instead of boredom I would delight in the daily clarity of sky and ocean, the quiet highway instead of city streets.

I always wonder how people act when they're alone. Does he pose and keep up a trivial running commentary for himself? Me, I try to act in public as I would like to be at all times—relaxed and peaceful. I don't like to show people my harried, worried, niggardly side because that can interest no one but myself.

Jon compliments my equanimity. Well, I recognize the inevitability of petty irritations; they're not worth the trouble of getting upset over.

Accept the potholes in the road—at least there is a road! Things could be worse, I say. I may have bad knees and hemorrhoids and a stopped up head and crabs, but I have two legs and a cock! I don't have cholera or the flu or even a cold.

Count your blessings, son! Appreciate what you have! No doubt Jon tells me so much because he likes me and wants to share his life here with me.

He loaned me his car for a drive up the mountain. Rimrock outcroppings in mesa-like steps, deep canyons with palms in the bottoms, brown hills a lot like the Sierra Nevada. Juan, a German friend of Jon's, says it's like the Yucatan. Small brick dams in gullies and mineral-smelling water. What appears to be sagebrush is not; when you get close it is a funny long-leafed plant. Played the rhaita where I thought nobody could hear—many echoes and at the tail end the sound of little bells over a hill.

The road is badly rutted and just wide enough for the Seat. I warned two tourists in a larger car at the top to turn back. They didn't, though. Maybe my Spanish was incomprehensible.

Lower down the other side are tall red brick walls along the road. The houses are made of fitted stone in pretty patterns. People stared at me.

Guanche is the name of the original inhabitants of the Canary Islands. They were tall with light skin, blue eyes, blond or reddish hair, and lived in caves. They were still here as late as the 1400s when Columbus passed through and stayed in Las Palmas at a house now called Casa de Colón. The only light-skinned people I saw were Europeans.

Chamomile tea is used both as a sedative and a cleansing solution for diaper rash. Firgas is a naturally carbonated mineral water from a spring in the north. I don't suppose tea is made from Firgas.

The accent drops all s's not vital to the comprehension of a word: Epagne, La Palma, pecado, papa frita.

Jon is a serious writer. Jon is a serious person who writes. Jon works hard. He sent himself to Exeter by selling more subscriptions to the Rocky Mountain News than any other paperboy.

When he had finally expressed enough apologies for the incompleteness of his novel, he gave me the first six chapters to read. Now I'm embarrassed. What can I say that won't offend him or hurt his feelings?

He's so proud of the tale of his wretched love affair. But where's the love? Hah! A love story by someone afraid of women. The poor sap doesn't know what love is. In college I hustled chicks in flares of passion, but his affairs were slow, staid beddings with dumpy future housewives. He described events like moves on a chessboard: What will happen if I do this, if she likes that or doesn't, ad nauseum. A mind caught in the sterile maze of analytical thought.

His chess game drives me nuts, he takes so long contemplating a move. I hardly bother to look at what he does—I just get in there and smash hell out of him. He's serious, slow, ponderous, thinks about all the possibilities and can't decide. I pick one and then another, try them all out. When he wins he's smug. When he loses he grudgingly tells me that I played well. Score: 4 me, 2 him. And I've taken a quarter of the time.

His characters must have felt more than he lets on, and nobody talks the way they do. They talk, the narrator talks, and it's all drivel. He needs to cut the verbiage and tell the story. What happened, what he felt. Actually, it's more a therapeutic exercise than storytelling—he writes to analyze what went wrong, to heal his own hurt.

It might sell to some teenage girl magazine if he cut one or two naughty words and the stabs at philosophizing, though they do show the main male character as a heartless analytical motherfucker. Jon portrays himself better than he realizes, an empty character with no concern for others. Not that he's malicious; it's a moral laziness, a blind defensiveness he's had since he was a backward and spectacled little boy who never quite caught on to what the big boys were doing.

He thinks creation is some magical thing that must be coaxed into the open. The artist is a privileged person who works hard for his privilege. I disagree. I think creation is the term applied to simple acts that anyone can do but doesn't get around to. And anyway, poems and paintings are play, not work. Someone may call your product a creation, but all you did was goof around. Furthermore, by inventing standards of creativity and righteousness to gauge himself against, he sets ghastly limits on what he values and what he allows himself to do. He falls into ruts and doesn't get as much out of life as he would if he simply opened his eyes and watched.

He has said twice, facetiously, that I am the only person he knows who is so crazy and smart, probably intending "crazy" as a rebuke and "smart" as camaraderie. I try to wed idea and action, intellect and senses. The best I can do is use them to their fullest.

How do you avoid boredom while major emotional changes or expansions of awareness are being prepared in the unconscious? Between great decisions (I will dodge the draft by moving to Europe; I will leave Europe and become a doctor; I love C and she loves me, woops, she loves me not) and their accomplishment, you have to occupy yourself. How do you incubate the growth, how pass the time in train stations?

Travel makes me marvel at the complexity and diversity of existence. Just seeing palm trees, banana plants, countryside covered by strange brush, huge lizards, brick dams, naturally carbonated mineral water, pebble houses, trees with perfectly symmetrical branches every two feet up the trunk, camels and horses yoked together for the plow—these make me feel good. They keep my imagination on its toes. Tales of the blue men of the Sahara, the sorcerers in the south, and possession by demons expand the possibilities in my own life.

Travel breaks down my resistance, my fears, my inhibitions. I gain self-confidence from getting around amidst foreign languages and customs. I can see the Cordillera, I can sit under a lotus tree in India, I can get into school or get a job at the mine in Telluride. I can do anything. I speak all languages, it's just that I haven't practiced most of them since the womb.

Some suggest that travel changes nothing in yourself that couldn't be changed while living in the same place. You drag around the same soul and you find the same problems everywhere. Do timid souls hid behind this thought? Because it takes some courage to travel. Often I hesitate before doing something because I don't know how it will be perceived. I don't know the customs, how to do it properly, and end up doing nothing at all but sit over the coupling of two train cars with a full bladder. Or I just run to the bathroom, walk up to a seat and plunk myself down, search for some damn thing in umpteen languages and gestures. (It's helpful being a foreigner because I can plead ignorance.)

Here on this tourist island are signs in Spanish, English, French, German, Norwegian, Danish, Finnish and Swedish and people who speak them. There are back roads to hamlets where people stare at me out of unelectrified huts. There is me blithering through, digging every funny or apprehensive moment of it. I'm alive to the roosters challenging each other across town. I learn how to enjoy every moment, even the sameness of the moments, the long stretches between the joyful moments of transition or awareness, because every moment is transition and awareness.

The rest of the time I keep busy (read, play guitar). I investigate my surroundings. I try to stay alive and aware between the infrequent moments of action and motion because unless I use the interim constructively, I will find that I have wasted the better part of my life.

Dear Lemming,

Of whose peregrine machinations is finally revealed the secret—the man who wanted to stick his cock up the cosmic cunt of creation— What? No, says he, I'm jus tryin ta find a better recipe for mulberry tarts, and you sir, would you care ta tell us your views on sex? THE YEWER'S BREAST MAKES THE BREED RISE. Thank you sir that wraps up the delousing struggle for today, now a quick word from our sponsor: Be happy, don't worry, let the Maya® Merry-Go-Round swing you through this life like the last!

Protect us from the arc between showerhead and corpus in Jon E's electrified shower chamber. In the East they say if you look deep enough into your own death you see the soles of your feet walking backwards. But the souls of your feet are frites in the heat of Jon's tortured chamber. No shower in the power, or it's the bower, boys.

I'm sitting on a hill on Gran Canaria's south side waiting for sunset. The westernmost reach of the Atlas range slouches off the continent into the Atlantic. It must be 90 degrees. Ringing blue sky and ocean, dazzling white walls which amplify my dry guitar. The fiendish maze of the chessboard between me and Jon. His poems and novel a tortured attempt to capture time, but he works so hard at it that only shells remain.

In five days I'll be in 30-degree Denver sloshing through the snow in sneakers to get into medical school.

Oakley's course in Getting It Together all over once again giving it all again the once-over. Row row rowing his barnacled boat back to port to rip the hoary bottom out and let the rime in.

I feel indebted to Jon. He has put me up for two weeks, given me money and lent me his car. But he expects me to feel indebted. The little prick could fall into the ocean on the way to work for all I care.

I'm sick and tired of talking about serious things. As soon as anything *must* be said I lose interest in saying it. I'm bored with the whole idea and want to leave.

But I'm trying not to be disagreeable. I keep my mouth shut most of the time, grin at his lame jokes, talk about the goddamn clouds and landscape.

More than anything I feel sorry for him. He is as dissatisfied with his situation as poor Youssef, who can't escape his restricted perceptions. Jon can, but wastes his opportunities by fitting perceptions into a static construct. In the end, his understanding is equally meager and his empathy is less. Which would seem to be a failing in a writer.

On the plane Las Palmas to New York. It is now 21:00 LPA, 16:00 JFK, 14:00 DEN. It is dusk and therefore about

17:30 here above the ocean. Where are we? Position as a function of time; position determined not by spatial but temporal coordinates.

We are all in this together. The flight crew, the passengers, the one-time student returning to Ohio from picking grapes in Spain for a French petit bourgeois overseer, the Americans on Big Dog playing with computers and satellites and manned flights to the moon, the Spanish tomato harvesters, the German tourists bronzing in the sun, the beer-drinking worker in the hotel where the scientists, technologists, and affluent meet to relax from propelling mankind upward, the lover blind to people while he paints the world in private colors.

Southward

After seven months with the railroad I'd saved two thousand dollars and decided to get serious about writing. I would hitchhike to San Francisco, visit friends, then head overland to Mexico, then El Salvador where my history teacher knew someone, through Central America and northern South America to French Guiana where I knew someone, and down the eastern coast to Rio where someone else had a friend. There I would find an apartment and hole up and write a second novel.

3 April 1974 San Diego
Flew here from San Francisco on auspicious April Fools' Day. Today I was sad talking with Mom and Dad for the last time but found comfort in knowing we will be in touch by mail. I will write, and can receive at Michel's place in Cayenne. Something to look forward to.

5 April
Yesterday the bus to Mexicali and the train south. The desert is boring. I don't know what comes next, but it must be better than barrel cactus, greasewood, dust and heat in the nineties, though even this is better than the boredom I've left. Wore my jacket against the chill last night; I'm looking forward to looking back on it as my last cool weather for many a year.

I can't understand the language but haven't died anywhere yet because of that.

Traveling, however, seems to have lost its magic and become simply the means of getting from one place to another. The sheer act of moving and seeing new things isn't as engaging as it was. Maybe I've mythologized travel because I was so bored. No: I remember the pleasure of new landscapes rolling into view. But this landscape is never new. Nothing in Denver was new, either.

I feel low in the evening; in fact, I feel low whenever I think backwards. I must look forward.

I will give myself $5 a day. That gives me a month to reach Cayenne with $300 in hand and $1,300 remaining in Denver. Not counting travel expenses, which are impossible to foresee. But $300 should get me from Cayenne to Rio. I shall figure that for every $5 spent en route I have one day less. I'll split the trip into stages; this stage takes me to Guiana. These thoughts make me feel better—forward-looking and planning for the future. As for the language, I'll make out the best I can.

This style reminds me of Stanley's in *How I Found Livingstone*. It is good—it sets me apart from myself, makes me objective.

6 April

The only place I've been where Spanish is spoken is Spain, so I've been surprised that this is not Europe. Gotta remember that it's Latin America, a new place.

Mexico does not feel like a foreign county. Zip you cross the border with no pain, no jet lag, as easy as crossing the street but they don't speak English and it's dirtier. I don't care for what I've seen. Of course, I've only seen Mexicali, this train, and Benjamin Hill for a two-hour layover to change trains. Dirty shacks crawling with dirty, serious children. Do all the little boys scowl?

7 April Mexico City

The monkey was a symbol of gaiety, laughter and love for the Aztecs but the thousands of people in Chapultepec Park are much less playful than the spider monkeys in the children's zoo. An impromptu audience did respond to an innovative rock group of three kids playing electric bass, a tiny guitar, and drums under the trees.

Maybe I'm feeling sour because I can't understand anything of this new culture and language. Though as I sit still and jot this, I feel the possibility of my mood improving.

Maybe I should come to a complete stop in, say, Costa Rica for a couple weeks and adjust more fully. It seems there is always this depression the first few days of any new thing. As long as the new thing is the overall journey I'll be okay since I'll get used to it, but if every new place brings the blues it'll wear me down.

I'm growing old. At least, I'm changing. I guess I no longer care for the hyperactive state of mind that travel induces and would rather be calm and relaxed. I have no self-confidence just now.

8 April Mexico City

Dreamed last night that I married a very plain girl. I regretted her lack of beauty but loved her and promised myself to never speak a word of regret.

Despite my insecurity, I give the impression of someone who knows what he's doing, someone who can take care of himself. I walked boldly into the Guatemalan consulate this morning and asked in Spanish for a visa, and understood that two photos and ten dollars were required for the visa but only one dollar for a tourist card, so I got the card. An American boy my age was completely lost. They told him he needed a smallpox vaccination to enter Guatemala. (They hadn't asked me about it.) I translated for him and got him the address of a clinic. He was a tall gangly puppy-dog fellow with glasses and a sophomore good boy haircut just touching the ears, a decent person, going to meet a veterinarian in Guatemala City.

I saw him later in a taxicab calling to a cop who called for an interpreter who talked to him for several minutes while I stood on the corner wondering if I should get involved. If I had joined him we could have spent the afternoon commiserating about how lonely and confusing it is to travel alone and talking about the crazy and confusing customs of Mexico City. I'd rather be on my own, though, because something more interesting than that might come up. I went to a post office and mailed postcards.

Rather than figure out the buses to the pyramids of Teotihuacán by myself, I decided to go on a packaged tour and dropped into a travel agency. It was friendship at first sight with the girl at the desk. Big warm brown eyes and a pretty, friendly face. I haven't seen many pretty girls here. She asked what I was doing and I told her my plans. She asked me to send her a postcard from Rio. I was going to ask her address but she had to take care of someone and while I waited had the idea of asking her out.

"Would you like to go to dinner tonight?"

"¿?"

"Quiere comer con miyo... esta... noche?"

"Oh si! Thank you, thank you!" Arrangements were made and I took off for Teotihuacán grinning like a baboon.

The pyramids were as spiffy as the Roman baths near Bordeaux. The Teotihuacáns had underground cisterns for water through the dry season and an advanced sewage system including even seats on the toilets. The city was large—seven miles by seven, the size of San Francisco—but when it burnt down the inhabitants left. I climbed the pyramid of the sun, larger than the pyramid of the moon, and stood in a strong wind chanting Om Shanti in all directions to commemorate my visit.

On the way back we visited the shrine of the Virgin of Guadalupe. I would have cried, since it meant so much to my mother, but didn't because of all the people. I should go back and do it on my knees but haven't the time. I must go forward.

Maria and I ate dinner. She said it was the first time she'd been out in three months! She is very sympathique. She spoke English and I spoke Spanish and English. Her English was better than my Spanish. She said I had sweet, tender eyes. She is a very nice girl, a friend, as she says. How wonderful.

She said I should visit Oaxaca and took me to the bus station for tickets but none were available for another four days. I bought one to San Salvador for Friday. Then she found me a cheaper room than the one where I'm staying.

I was worried about getting her home before it was too late, and deeply appreciated her help with the bus and the hotel, but hadn't the vocabulary to say what I felt, though I think she understood, as I understood all she tried to say. The conversation was most difficult and hesitating, but we liked each other and shook hands warmly at the entrance to her subway stop.

I want to leave here. It's too much like home without the palliative of novelty. There are no doubt good places to be found but my direction is south. I must arrive in Rio with $1,000 remaining in Denver, preferably with $1,300. Because what if I don't like Rio and want out? Let's not think like that. It's hard to shake this depression. It seems to be abating, but I don't want to hope for fear of scaring off improvement. Superstition.

If I got an alarm clock I'd be more in control.

9 April Mexico City

I compared the cost of air fare to Guatemala to the expense of waiting here until Friday plus four days' overland travel, trying to decide if I want to stay long enough to visit Oaxaca or go now to Guatemala or skip it and El Salvador too and fly directly to Costa Rica.

Maria and I drank coffee and talked the evening away. I like her company though we barely understand each other. I've been walking so much that my eyes are bruised with fatigue and my ankles ache like never before and I've been living mainly on cigarettes. Must get two or three days of rest. I'm starting to enjoy things in weird moments of physical, animal contentment. All this exercise is destroying my capacity to analyze, though I can still collect impressions. Looking forward to a vacation on the beach in Costa Rica. The thought came to elaborate on the idea of death as one's best friend.

What am I doing traveling around like this? Must find out the return fare from Rio and be sure to set it aside.

Ce pays me fait chier et je tiens à sortir le plus vite possible. A bunch of laughing children were running and shouting in the park; then a little boy tried to push a little girl into the fountain. A sullen people with chips on their shoulders. See DH Lawrence *The Plumed Serpent* and Octavio Paz *The Labyrinth of Solitude*. Maria is an exception.

And J, my sweet brother. No hardness in him. If he is rebuffed by other kids, he is saddened without understanding why. I feel paternal as well as fraternal. I wonder if I was like him.

Things I have seen: Chapultepec Park and Castle, Museo Nacional de la Antropología, Museo del Arte Moderno (two by my mother's brother-in-law Alfredo Zalce), Museo de las Bellas Artes, Teotihuacán, the church of the Virgin of Guadalupe, Plaza de la Constitución, the Spanish baroque Catedral Metropolitan, Palacio Nacional, subway stop with Aztec altar, *Take the Money and Run* by Woody Allen with Maria, who was more puzzled than amused.

Paintings by Daniel Siqueiros: ghastly figures of horror, inquisitions, blood, revolution, deformities. Fascism is hardest on sensitive persons. H Bosch, Shostakovich. Bosch must have seen what Siqueiros saw but he painted in the idiom (religious) of his time.

The main theme of modern Mexican painting is pride in bondage. Tortured cubist people struggling to wrench free. The Indian denied his identity. Complete submission. The mestizo.

Maybe the mestizo symbolizes the problem. The Mexicans are trying to characterize their culture, define it, by searching through their various myths to take what fits. There is a big push for awareness of the Indian and Spanish Catholic mix. But the approach isn't broad enough—they don't see themselves in relation to the rest of the world. Cultural self-identity has always been grounded in a chauvinist view and sense of superiority to other cultures. Consider the Greeks, Germans, Americans, British, US Black Consciousness, etc. It is time to supersede this by developing an awareness of self that comprises our relations to all things in the universe.

Which brings us to *El Hombre Controlador del Universo,* Diego Rivera 1934, in the Museo de las Bellas Artes. At the center is a blond man surrounded by machinery and scientific instruments and glory, his hands on the atom, the chromosome, the galaxies and fertile plants, but he is alone, lonely, resignation and acceptance on his face, blue eyes almost starting to be forced shut by the vision of the power he is experiencing, eyes darkly ringed by manly fatigue.

Surrounding him are the idle rich, the hungry and poor, the powerless people who want power and will destroy and kill and maim for it. Their eyes hold greed and hatred and sly grasping. They would rip apart the idle rich and tear through the machinery and trample on babies to reach the center of power, hands clawing aside the faces of their comrades, and when they arrive they will find this humble man alone, unable to resist or even notice their arrival because power is in him and has taken him for itself. He can no more turn his eyes or remove his hands from the controls as someone at the center of the sun and ocean and sky and earth can open his mouth to speak. He is the green fuse through which the force drives the flower.

He is the god-man, the modern myth, the expression of today's world culture. He is for us what Faust was for the ogival civilization, Apollo-Dionysos for the Greeks, Ra for the Egyptians. He is the Hero. He would turn, if he could move, with resignation and acceptance and wonder to his woman and they would mate and be one still point in the splendor, one omniscient incorporation of flower and nebula.

That is what I would like it mean.

The sign said: This is a replica of a mural with the same theme done at the Rockefeller Center in New York but destroyed for political reasons. Rivera hace la apología del hombre controlando mecanicamente el universo. And it said that he had a great respect and love for the sciences.

Two ellipsoids crossing behind el controlador represent the macrocosm (planets and stars) and the microcosm (blood cells, entrails, zygotes). Beneath him are fertile plants, fruit, vegetables, roots, geological strata, fossils, springs, petroleum.

On the left are decadent capitalists who profit from the power controlled by the blond man, from repression, hunger strikes, and the gas-masked soldiers marching toward workers on the right. The workers' faces show horror, but their flags fly as they march to the encounter. Lenin stands behind them clasping together the hands of workers of all races and sexes. He gazes off the canvas, focused on a goal as yet unachieved and thus unrepresentable—but his look is political, not transcendent like el hombre's.

No one looks at el controlador; they may not even know he exists though they have probably heard rumors. Their vision is much lower, on the news and on each other. Only an x-ray skull grins at him—Death, who sees us all.

Charles Darwin in the lower left looks at the spectator as he points to the animals (including a baby) who are evolutionary precedents to man. How could this mural have been destroyed for political reasons, with Darwin giving the clue? The main theme is the evolution of man. Socialism and capitalism are not man's apex—they are only expressions of contemporary social order.

On the left is a large statue of Zeus Updated—he wears a cross and his thunderbolts come from a Van de Graaf generator. On the right is the statue of a headless figure grasping a fasces held together by a band with a swastika. The statue is bullet-pocked, and workers are sitting on its head in the lower right, fascism and Stalinism (perverted forms of socialism) having been superseded by the Fourth International.

10 April Mexico City

My Spanish is improving. Maria says I now speak it better than she does English. I don't know about that, but give me two more weeks.

I'm growing accustomed to Mexico City, but the people are not to my taste.

17 April Playa Manuel Antonio, Quepos, Costa Rica

It has cost $250 to get from San Diego to here. I gotsa lotsa moola left. And the closer to Rio I come, the less I worry. I guess I want to get straight to where I'm going with no detours. Learn to play piano in three days. A language in a week. I was too impatient to spend time in Oaxaca or take train and bus so I flew to San José. Beautiful people, unlike Mexico—must be the addition of Chinese to the mix. Some

American kids said Quepos had a good beach, so here I came in a drafty old DC-3 that landed on a dirt airstrip in the jungle. I'm staying in a hammock at an easy-going restaurant a hundred feet from the ocean. There are other young people but not many because the rainy season is beginning.

It is extraordinarily pretty when not cloudy: blue blue sky and green sea, green foliage. Birds, crabs, insects. My legs are quite bitten but they don't itch much. Overwhelming sub-physical low for a couple days due to lack of food, seawater in inner ears, heat and humidity. Sunburned feet and shoulders.

Whenever I start feeling very bad, I take a dip in the warm ocean, have a shower and eat something. I feel better afterwards, though I haven't been on top of things since I left San Francisco.

Had a gut-wrenching memory this morning of what it is like to work for wages, especially the first week or two. Maybe I will look for work in Maracaibo on the drilling rigs.

I have absolutely no idea what I'm doing.

These traveling kids are not very interesting. At best, conversation is a comparison of different personalities and from there it ranges downward to gossip, drug talk, and stoned chatter. Since it always includes travel plans and suggestions of where to go, the same people meet at the same places. There are a lot of ugly loud-mouths.

The other night it rained, so I hopped from the hammock to T and L's Toyota. Soon M and her lover for the night appeared and M said, "Oh! You're here."

"Hello," said I, "there's room for three."

They didn't say anything and left, but soon M woke me again. "I'm sorry, but T and L said I could sleep in here if it rained, and it doesn't look like it's going to quit." T and L had also told me I could sleep there if it rained. "Do you want a sleeping bag?" she said. An ultimatum if I ever heard one.

I piled out to avoid an argument with her and her lover for the night, found the bag, and slept on a table in the restaurant.

The traveling girls use sex as a weapon. They're brazen in dress, carriage, and talk and bestow their pussy on whomsoever it pleaseth them. Requisite is a deep tan, possession of drugs, and sycophantic flattery. The guys are horny so they cater to the girls. I wouldn't mind a little sex but hate to lower myself to that level.

The Sound and the Fury and *Gravity's Rainbow,* contact with the world beyond this island of Circe.

21 April Cahuita

At the beach I met a journalist who had fled Argentina and his Colombian girlfriend, who invited me to stay with them in San José. She made empañadas for a vendor, always singing, happy to be with him, while he typed in the living room. I helped with the empañadas but mostly stayed in my room studying Spanish and reading and writing letters about my impressions and my aim to write books, each book a contribution to the body of thought and beauty created by the best minds across the centuries, or failing that, to make my life a work of art (perhaps a nobler goal). What would be a life lived artfully? Each moment a pearl on the string that was myself within the harmonious weave of nature, each instant savored so that what remained of life no matter how long or short would be dessert, an unnecessary but delightful prolongation of this banquet spread before us all... Until she very kindly told me that they were worried about me holed up in my room and I should get out more. So I took a train to the Caribbean where the traveling kids said there was good snorkeling at a reef off a town named Cahuita.

I hadn't slept much for a couple nights and rode along with low energy, language paranoia, hunger. I bought a tostada through the window at a station and was eating it bent forward between my knees to avoid spilling juice on my pants when the train lurched, I rocked forward and back, slightly peeved knowing I should do something fast, and when my face shot forward into the seat I had just enough time to berate my stupidity at not having acted. The train stopped. I stayed bent forward to avoid spilling blood on my pants, fought off unconsciousness, felt my nose which seemed to have something loose inside, realized there had been a wreck, fought to stay aware and conscious. Passed out. Came to as if an act of will dragged me from a nightmare in which my lungs were so full I couldn't exhale, thought I was in Colombia or fallen out of the car with the cream cheese when I was three in South Dakota, my father bent over me and then my mother holding me, incomprehensible heat, saw the jungle and heard shouting and remembered Costa Rica and very far from Mom and Dad and must take care of myself. All paranoia vanished and I relaxed and bled and sat until I felt I could go get water to rinse my face, which I did and came very close to passing out on the way back, holding on to other seats. A woman gave me alcohol-soaked cotton to swab my face. The skin between lip and nose was split and it would be three or four days before I could dive. Two front teeth were sore but not chipped or loose. I was not permanently damaged. I laughed now and then to think that I had been in a train wreck in Costa Rica on this ancient roller coaster.

People were giving first aid to the injured. We backed up, so I knew we hadn't derailed, and stopped again in the station. The last bit of my tostada was on the floor in a puddle of blood. A passenger train pulled alongside. We looked at each other and people talked to me but I understood little. I did understand that our sudden stop had been to avoid a head-on collision.

Off we started and in twenty minutes stopped in a larger town. A woman selling tostadas to the window ahead saw my face and talked at length to me but I understood nothing. A crowd of people, mostly kids, came to my seat and I understood that I could go to the hospital. I didn't want to delay reaching Limón, so I said I'd stay on the train. They left but returned with a fireman. I caught the words *seguro social* which I took to mean insurance and thought briefly of a cash settlement and then that I was probably required to fill out forms which made me give up and go. An ambulance took me to a hospital where a journalist took a picture of my sheepishly smiling bloody face. There were many people. Someone had a broken leg. I waited, gave my name, got a tetanus shot and a stitch in my nose without anesthetic, then walked back to the station instead of waiting for a ride. Next train was in an hour.

When it got dark the train was dark, and outside was black jungle, fireflies, lightning, cloudbursts, howling monkeys. Several unannounced stops. Once the brakeman set the handbrake of my car and I heard *máquina mala* which figured. I chuckled a lot and stayed in high spirits. All I had was a broken nose.

I arrived twelve and a half hours after leaving, rather a long time to go 180 kilometers. I had planned on staying the night in Limón but it seemed simpler to get into a car which was heading south just then. We were switched back and forth to the rear of a new train, amusing because in the US it's illegal to switch cars with passengers on board. I told the switchman-conductor that I wanted off at the town with the boat to the bus that went to Cahuita. The town's name is Penshurt, I later learned, also Penshurst and Penhurst; they are all used. I couldn't stay awake. The conductor woke me in a pitch black cloudburst and shined his lamp at a building and said there was no hotel but I might try there for accommodations. I dashed through the rain and in the quick flash of my last match made out a bench at the back of a veranda, took out my contact lenses, brushed my teeth, listened to people snoring in the dark all around, and slept until early dawn pinked the river behind the shacks. Took up my luggage and hailed a canoe from the other bank, stood with several others in the nervous hull, and scrabbled up a mud bank to board the waiting bus for the last ten kilometers.

Cahuita is a small black town where life is slow. Two general stores. No matches to be had. Bread comes from Limón. The only pastime is chess, which even the children play. No musical instruments. Many gringos. When the first ones came three years ago, the locals thought their surfboards were beds. The Latin natives speak Spanish, the blacks a melodic English patois which I imagine was spoken in the deep South a century ago, but with Spanish words thrown in. There is talk of cheap land for sale. I've been bitten by the fever; if I can get a little land for a couple hundred dollars I shall.

Since I can't wear a mask to dive because of my cut lip, I walked shirtless much too far along the beach and burnt my shoulders to the point of blistering. Stupid. Now I can't dive until that heals, too. But a flying fish skipped like a silver oblong stone in long catenaries just beyond the breaking waves.

24 April

The gringos:

A Texan whose 22nd birthday is today has bought 18 hectares for $1,300. Has a horse. I haven't seen him sober yet. He is obnoxious and now that he has land, he's telling the natives not to sell for low prices because there will be a boom.

A tall awkward Bible-beater who has a high opinion of himself but lacks social graces. He was with missionaries in Colombia, then two years in Chicago's inner city with black kids, and is studying Spanish in San José to prepare himself to work with Colombian kids. "You must come to grips with the resurrection of Christ. Accepting this, you must understand the rest." I didn't ask what the rest was.

Graham talks tough and drinks a lot. "If you haven't drunk guaro, you haven't drunk." He continually rags on Sloane Kee, the Chinese owner of one of the general stores. He schemes how to gyp a native out of a colon but spends as much as my daily allowance each night on beer and junk food.

A group in from the surrounding area are drinking at a table in Sloane's big dance room, getting noisier, playing Bob Dylan, Santana, sixties American rock on the jukebox.

Some gringos are apparently trying to start farms. Others are land speculators. They try to impress everybody and stay at the center of attention. Their insensitive and overpowering attitude seems to be introducing a new element of hardness, of tough cool—the older natives are soft-spoken but the younger blacks in contact with the gringos use heavy obscenity. This is colonization. How sad that first come the misfits, the plain bums who can live here cheap, and the bullies seeking places where their quirks aren't known yet, where their first-world wealth makes them big fish. Five boys to each girl. They really are dissipated sadsacks who couldn't even get a girl to come with them.

Tourist places are not good places, for the lives of tourists and natives don't meet. Local life boils in grottos and channels and scorns the mist passing overhead, and the mist flows around the rocks and knows it belongs to the air and not the earth and soon floats off on the wind searching for other places.

In general the natives put up with it.

Sloane Kee owns the larger general store, a Toyota pickup and a Chevy pickup, and a Land Rover and two dump trucks in Limón which constitute a transportation company. I'm staying in a room above the store. He's affable but sometimes seems exasperated with the Americans. He's sharp. He asked me the reason for a national park. I told him it was to keep the land from being developed. Instant comprehension. He has land to sell on the beachfront behind the new park. He offered me an acre for $900 or a hectare in town for $4,000. Too bad I haven't the money. He at once offered credit. He's not avaricious, knows the value of things and can see the future. In twenty years he will own the town.

Miss Anita runs a restaurant, which consists of two tables in her living room. "Sit down honey, I'm coming." She finishes her chat with an old fisherman before shuffling round the porch to the kitchen to get your plateful of rice, beans, barbecued pollo and fried bananas and coffee. Fat, middle-aged, dark, slow, scrupulously honest. "One seventy, honey," she tells me what I owe. I give her one seventy-five. "I just check if you give me more." She counts. "You get five change. Wait I go get it." Breakfast is French toast with molasses and fried bananas. She's an affable lady: she laughed heartily when she gave me two knives and a tablemate two forks. For okay she says "Check," or, "Dat's okay honey."

The head of the political district is getting his cocoa farm in shape to support himself completely and then he'll quit politics.

Wood or cement pilings hold the houses off the ground. Many places are barely a bunch of boards nailed together. Few of the windows have glass or screens, though there are wooden shutters to close at night, which must be for visual privacy since sound and mosquitoes easily pass through the walls. Roofs are tin.

The town is a hot, humid, easy-going place. It closes from noon to two or three. People are only active from dawn to just after dusk. Electricity from dusk to midnight or so. There is a school. No cars; the only vehicle I've seen is Sloane's pickup, though I saw a dump truck once, and four or five times a day the Puerto Viejo–Penshurt bus comes to town.

I've relaxed enough to peacefully watch the sea and read for hours. Tico beggars come and start a drunken conversation. If somebody tells you how much he likes Americans, he's going to ask for money. Though one lady bought me Vaseline for my sunburn (with my money) before she asked for two colons. They keep coming back whether I've donated or not.

26 April

Today the first TV antenna in Cahuita was installed on Sloane Kee's roof.

Since I couldn't snorkel, I accepted an invitation from a young local to go fishing for two dollars. We pushed his boat off the beach and rowed out a hundred meters. He baited a hook with a piece of fish and handed me the pole. I enjoyed the view of the coast and expected nothing, but damned if I didn't land a silvery fish some two feet long. He took the pole but had no luck and after an hour we returned. I offered him the fish but he refused, saying I had caught it. "But what do I do with it?" I asked. He shrugged.

Well, I had wanted to eat lobster but couldn't afford it, so I took the fish to Miss Anita and traded it for a lobster dinner. I don't know what she did with it, but she got a lobster from somewhere and cooked it for me that evening. She probably made a killing on the deal and I was happy for her. Alas, the lobster wasn't all that good.

28 April
Rain foiled my plan to dive so I played chess with some gringos. Most are not malicious and one or two might actually be decent, but they are all brash, ignorant and insensitive.

I could invent a character who chooses to die rather than live in an insensitive world.

We Americans have our hackles up when we meet someone new, and it's normal to be guarded until we know we can trust someone, but there's no reason to be afraid, no reason to assume someone thinks badly of you. It's easy to get friendly with someone. Smile, they smile back. It's the same with new situations, new jobs, new places. Walk around, gauge the reactions of the natives to a newcomer (almost always at least toleration), you fit in fast.

1 May
I finally snorkeled. The tide was low and the swell lifted and lowered me to within a foot of the reef, which was just lovely with colorful fishes and lobsters. I found myself above a bed of urchins with hard, sharp spines tranquilly aimed at my chest. When the water dropped I held my breath for buoyancy and my body straight and rigid, and when the swell rose I carefully turned and kicked slowly back to safety. I began to think I was not fated to dive that reef.

6 May San José
I returned to San José thinking I should move on to Rio. The Argentine convinced me that Buenos Aires is more cosmopolitan. Plus, I won't have to learn Portuguese. So now that's my goal.

How good I feel! Even with bad language paranoia or gut-twisting incertitude about something as silly as what to wear, although my alien status is difficult and sometimes crushing, it's all good: It's my own life, not a fictional one I try to emulate or one constrained by school or a meaningless job. I've made a good start. I could return to the US where I'd be high and self-confident (for a couple months) but my life is coming into my own hands and I want to see where this takes me.

Preserve your options; don't burn your bridges behind you—my dad.

Know thyself—the Greeks.

Moderation in all things—the Greeks.

…including moderation—me.

Better to regret having done something than regret not having done it—the girlfriend who left home to live with the man she fell in love with. She asked me to deliver a letter to her twin sister in Bogotá, since their parents would intercept it if it came in the mail.

10 May Isla de San Andrés, Colombia

The travelers' network said San Andrés was a good place to snorkel. It is a free port and tourist resort with casinos and expensive hotels but I found a room in the poor part of town.

11 May

I overcame my shyness and got a haircut at a barber shop up the street and then snorkeled at the beach to rinse off. Checked out the casinos and tourist shops. I don't fit in anywhere.

12 May

Suppose you get an urge for popcorn one afternoon on the beach as the breeze comes up. You're not sure if the last popcorn you saw was in Mexico City or San Francisco. Me, I crave popcorn three or four times a year, but it goes away if I ignore it. I learned to do that the first time I was challenged to stop after one potato chip (though it wasn't that hard since I never cared for them). Well, there was no way in hell that I'd be merrily crunching away at a bag of kernels within the next five minutes, so I resigned myself to a glass of pineapple juice.

Which brings me to mangos. For twenty-three years I didn't crave mangos. I couldn't very well, could I, since I'd never tasted one.

Well now, that First Bite! You peel the skin and scrape it with your teeth like you eat an artichoke and your mouth fills with the fragrance of fir! You suddenly exhale a forest of mountain evergreens. Finish the skin and glom the fruit in your mouth for bigger and fatter mouthfuls until you reach the sticky taffy-string leavings on the pit. It's heaven!

My sense of tidiness and order came into play at the end of the feast and I glanced surreptitiously around to see how others disposed of their pits. For the first time I examined the litter in the streets and saw seeds and rinds and pits. I'd written the trash off to a lack of civic conscience or sanitation infrastructure, but then I saw another way of looking at it. If fruit like this is there for the plucking or the cost of a mere two cents, why work any harder than you must? I tossed it over my shoulder like a native.

That was in Cahuita, and it was a while before I ate another. You see, I liked that mango so much I was afraid I would get used it. What if I started craving them like popcorn? What if I were in Cheyenne, say, and got the urge? Offhand I don't know where you will find one within a thousand miles. This is a problem for the traveler: In the Caribbean you can't get popcorn and at home you can't get mangos.

Okay, so I was skin diving off the beach when a local named Octavio came up and asked if I wanted to row out to some really good diving spots. He took me on a tour of the huge barrier reef with splendid colorful fish, manta rays, lethal-looking barracudas which he assured me were harmless. Rowing was hot and the sun was fierce, and I was terribly thirsty though I didn't want to admit it before he did. Then he handed me a mango.

I gave up. I eat mangos like mad. Damn the cravings, full speed ahead!

13 May

Now it's off to Bogotá where I must write and submit to magazines and newspapers. I probably won't see mangos again for a long time. May I not start craving potato chips.

Too bad I'm leaving. After three days I've learned my way around and picked up enough to quit feeling totally uneasy, jumpy, bored, and wishing I had a real and solid life. I could do some good diving with Octavio, really learn how, but I'm leaving tomorrow because I made the plans during yesterday's paranoia, and I've spent an extravagance on food and gambling and movies. My allowance is depleted. So yet again I leave when I'm just starting to break through.

15 May Cartagena

Saw the colonial port and castle I came to see, walked all day, exchanged $40 for pesos at twice the official rate with a guy on the street. He counted out 2,000 in several hundred-peso notes, some fifties and twenties and many fives, and handed me the thick wad. The breakdown seemed odd, so I started counting from the fives on the outside. He snatched it back and recounted, and it came to 2,000 again. I was still suspicious but we were in a crowd and I didn't want to prolong exposing how much money I had so I put it in my pocket. He turned and vanished. With a sinking feeling I returned to my room. There were many fives and nothing else. The instantaneous loss of a week's living expenses was a blow. I told myself it was tuition for a lesson in trusting my instincts.

18 May Bogotá

I delivered the letter to the very kind, appreciative and beautiful sister happy for news of her eloped twin, spent a short hour in their parents' house in a gated community with the taxi waiting outside while she read it and thanked me and gave me tea and cookies. Went back to the city, walked around, saw *Les Patineurs* performed by a Canadian company before a talkative audience munching popcorn. Didn't crave it.

19 May

As I walked alone up a road at the edge of the city, three young guys ran up and demanded my wallet. I resisted but one showed a knife so I said okay take it, take it, okay, but leave my papers. They had the grace to take only the ten dollars in my wallet and also a ballpoint pen and might have taken more but a man in a business suit ran toward us with a pistol in his hand. The bandits ran down the hill as he fired at them, pow pow, pow—should I run away before he returns to shoot me?—turned out he was a cop and told me to file a complaint at the station, maybe my money would be recovered. I was called in the next day for a lineup of six men being beaten with a rubber truncheon and identified one of them. What happened to him? Did he go to prison? Did the others deserve to be beaten?

28 May Denver

An overwhelming feeling of rootlessness set in, and I had run through my money much faster than planned. I'd had enough of traveling, enough of adapting to a new place every few days, wanted to go to settle down in a place, get to know the place and settle myself down. Where? I didn't know the language in Rio, knew it only passably in Buenos Aires, just fine in Paris and San Francisco, already had friends in San Francisco, otherwise they were all the same. San Francisco it was. I wired my parents to send half my money and bought gifts for the family and the cheapest ticket to the States I could find, which landed me in Miami, where I got a Drive-away car to Memphis.

Exaltation overcame me driving through the green, English-speaking South.

I was free.

The question of freedom typically arises when one cannot do what he wishes. I was a white male middle-class American with an education, a degree and money in the bank, and I was presentable enough to get a job when it ran out. I could do whatever I wished.

My question was: What shall I use my freedom for?

The answer was: To work. To apply myself, to get engaged in something, to build.

When we produce nothing, we float from whim to whim and fad to fad and never realize our potential. I had feared that committing myself to one course would preclude others. As it certainly does. But potential is nothing until it is used. Freedom is squandered when it is not exercised. Unless I committed to one of my talents—any talent, pick one—I would become a bum among all the others on the beach.

I'd floated long enough. It was time to grow roots.

Down the River to Manaus

Well, boys, here's how it is:
I'm in a hospital in Manaus recuperating from exposure and an American lady was kind enough to loan me her typewriter. I'm a center of attraction, which isn't surprising since not much seems to happen here in the jungle.

You can't imagine the jungle.

I got to Bogotá on May 16, hoping to find work at the international commercial fair there in July. I'd been told that translators make good money at the fair and that francophones are at a premium. But after a couple days I decided I didn't care for Bogotá. It has its good points, I'm sure, but its bad points were too many. The weather is cold, the poverty is dangerous (I was robbed twice), theater audiences are obnoxious, the city looks like it has been bombed out.

I flew to Leticia on the 20th. That is a river town. The jungle there makes the jungles of Costa Rica look like a city zoo. The only way in or out is by plane or boat and let me tell you, neither is very sure. The first thing I saw was the wreckage of a plane that had crashed while landing three days earlier. Same airline I was flying, too. As for boats, they're tree-trunk canoes used by the Indians to go up the river to Iquitos in Peru or down to various small towns on the Solimões. A mailboat comes up from Manaus twice a month, and there are a few small johnboats with outboards that belong to rubber growers and three or four packets that belong to the town boss.

People told me that your plans of spending time in Leticia depend on whether the boss likes you or not. I was planning on being there just long enough to get out, but the mailboat had left two days before and wasn't due for another twelve.

There is nothing to do in town except be robbed, and living is expensive since everything is flown or boated in. I didn't want to wait two weeks or meet the boss, so I made leaving my main conversational topic. In one of the bars I got to talking with a fellow with Indian relatives who had come up the river from their home in Brazil to trade and would be going back in a day or two.

We found the four of them that evening, got good and drunk, looked at their canoes and so forth. They agreed to take me downriver as far as their village, Puriana, which is some hundred miles east of the confluence of the Juruá. From there to Manaus would be only 200 or 250 miles, and I could find someone in the village to take me the rest of the way. The price was a cigarette lighter and twenty Colombian pesos, about two bucks.

The next day I bought more cigarette lighters, cans of fluid, a hammock and a mosquito net. I got my passport taken care of at the Brazilian Consulate. They counseled against going and encouraged me to wait for the mailboat if I was so set on going by river.

Nowadays I would take advice like that. I've learned more about life in the back woods. But I had too much pride or something equally stupid, like faith in my good luck, though it had never been tested against anything worse than getting to a bus station on time or finding a job or apartment. The advice might have been reasonable for your average tourist, but I was the product of an advanced civilization with a quick, trained mind capable of working through any problems that arose. Well, my mind worked well enough, but the problems turned out to require not so much mind power as the good sense which would have kept me from going in the first place. But give up traveling in canoes down the Amazon? Hey, this was adventure!

Well, now I know better about adventures.

We spent eight days and seven nights traveling. By day we kept far away from shore where the bugs didn't go. It was boring and sitting all day made me ache. Toward dusk we headed for shore and I strung up my hammock and net, mostly staying inside away from the bugs and coming out to eat when the meal was ready. It was rice and whatever fish had been caught. I did a lot of the fishing since the four Indians, two in each canoe, paddled. When we saw another canoe, they would hail it in Indian, and sometimes the other occupants spoke a different dialect.

At night there were unknown grunts and howls and shuffling and always a deafening drone of bugs. You had to raise your voice to be heard. It was incredible but the Indians didn't seem to mind, so I pretended I didn't notice.

All four of them spoke some Portuguese and one a little Spanish. It was very hard to communicate. Given our cultural differences, there wasn't much to talk about anyway besides the weather and distances and prices of things. Even so, I could recognize their four personalities and some group dynamics by the time we got to Puriania.

I stayed in the house (under the roof) of one of the guys in my canoe and passed the time practicing chess, fishing, and getting sick of manioc and fish. The mosquitoes, fleas, ants, lice, horseflies, and other bugs were bad, but I was getting used to them. I played with the children a lot. Having nobody to talk to teaches you to amuse yourself, that's for sure.

A rubber collector would arrive one of these days and I could go downstream with him, but he kept not showing up. After five days I was getting worried about not being alive by the time he got there. The good times were passing. Most of the people were okay—they ignored me—but six or seven men were very unpleasant. I'm too tired now to describe the situation; believe me that I felt real danger in staying much longer.

I did some hard talking and two days later two kids agreed to take me down to Manaus for four cigarette lighters and all the fluid, plus fifty cruzeiros and a bottle of vodka when we got there. I could see that their hearts weren't in it; they didn't really want to go. Pushing was a mistake, but I sure as heck wanted out of there.

So we left early one morning for the five day trip. They didn't talk much except to mutter to each other. At dusk of the second day they seemed uneasy. By noon of the third day I realized they were lost. I figured it out myself, since they spoke only a few words of Portuguese and were ignoring me completely by then. If they were worried there was cause for worry, but I figured they were the best people to be with if you're going to be lost in the Amazon.

Here's something I didn't appreciate: This river is huge. There are other huge rivers coming in as well as scores of small ones. There are thousands of islands. The country is flat, so in some places there are many channels with many curves. Some channels were half a mile wide but they tell me here in Manaus that many are unnavigable even in a canoe because of aquatic vegetation.

That's where we were, in channels, and we spent most of the afternoon heading back upstream as they examined entrances to other channels. Two hours before sundown they chose one of them, hesitantly it seemed, and headed along it until dusk. Actually, I don't know if they were lost or not; it could have been staged. That evening they wouldn't talk to me. They ate in sullen silence and turned in to their hammocks right away. Me too. By then I was mighty worried.

When I woke up in the morning they were gone.

Well boys, I said to myself, that's that. I had the clothes I was wearing—a pair of long pants, underpants, and a short-sleeved shirt—my hammock and mosquito net and a small canvas bag containing my valuables: money, papers, camera, toothbrush, glasses, a Spanish-Portuguese dictionary. I always slept with that bag. I don't know why they didn't kill me and take it.

The old quick, trained mind came to the fore and reasoned that I was on my own, so I didn't waste time waiting for my friends or anybody else to come by. I worked a log loose from the underbrush beside the river and broke off most of the branches, slung the bedding around my torso and looped the strap of the bag over a branch, climbed on, pushed off, and rolled over. The bag was gone. One thing less to worry about, I thought, though for eyesight all I had left were the contacts I was wearing.

There isn't much to the art of navigating a log, because you can't. I spent hours and hours untangling the damn thing when it got stuck in foliage. I got mighty hungry. When night fell it was black. I'd been planning to rest on shore, but I was in a current further out and floated all night. I could lie in a certain position on my back if I didn't move. I got really stiff. Couldn't sleep, because I had to stay awake enough to keep from tipping over. Though the air and water were warm, I got chilled. I was glad to see the sun finally come up, but the transition from chill to warmth to fierce heat was rapid and the heat was as bad as the chill. At least there was water to drink.

I didn't think about much. Chance in a million of living through it. All I knew was that Manaus was downstream, and that was the way I was heading. I thought about everything that could go wrong. Thought about piranhas. Et cetera. After a while I wasn't thinking so much as being numb. I tried to keep the hammock over me against the sun but most of my attention was on keeping my balance and not losing the hammock and net.

That evening the trunk got hung up in a huge mass of water lilies. Impossible to get through. I fell off tangled in the net and just about drowned. I was so weak I didn't think I was going to get free. I did, though. By then the current, though slow, had carried me too far from the log to hang on and rest. It was only ten yards away, but that was too far. Swimming in the water lilies was impossible.

I can't describe the ordeal it was getting to shore. I was so weak I could hardly keep my head up, and I couldn't swim, and the lilies weren't solid enough to support me. And I had an insane fear of unknown animals in the water. And it was getting dark.

There wasn't a shore, just swamp. I wasn't strong enough to climb a tree but managed to pull myself into the crook of two fallen trunks and collapse. Couldn't even worry about caimans. I tried to shield my face from bugs. Got my contacts out and wrapped in a bill in my pocket. I sort of slept and sort of didn't. I was getting a fever.

By morning my exposed skin was puffy with bites. I was past misery, I'll tell you, just sort of aware that the sun had come up and not sure if I wanted to move. But I could die if I just lay there. I would simply fade out.

I put my contacts back in so I could see. My eyes hurt with them in, but then everything hurt and it didn't matter. I saw where I was. About a hundred yards downstream the water lilies ended. A good thing. I crawled, sloshed and stumbled that far. If it had turned out that there were more of them, I probably would have stopped and croaked. But there was open water.

I heard a motorboat pass on the river but couldn't see it. Didn't bother to shout. It was sort of heartbreaking.

By midafternoon I had rigged three thin logs together with my pants. Thin logs were all I could push around. I waded out until the water was deep and floated off. Then I found I didn't have the strength to pull myself onto the logs. I worked an arm under the pants so I didn't have to hold on. Then the pants loosened and the logs came apart. I hung on to one with just my head above water. This probably happened pretty fast.

My hands were numb. I didn't care much any more. Then a boat came over. It was a cabin cruiser with two Royal Dutch Shell employees and their wives on an outing. I found that out later.

People keep saying it was a miracle. Could be. I don't believe in divine intervention. It happened, is all, and if it hadn't, it wouldn't have. But if miracle means so unlikely as to be impossible, then it was a miracle.

Well, they got to Manaus in the middle of the night. I was totally out of it. I wasn't asleep but in a bad nightmare. I knew I was safe but it didn't mean anything. I got my contact lenses out. You know, for the past several hours all I had done was concentrate on one thing at a time, like taking the contacts out or putting them in or untangling myself from that damned mosquito net. Bad dreams. Chills.

    I was aware of being brought to the hospital. They told me I was unconscious for two days. I remember being feverish. It was as though once I was safe, I let down all my defenses and let the fever come. Though I guess I was at the point of letting them all down safe or not.

    Then I was weak for a couple days. Officials interviewed me and talked about hunting for the two Indians, but it doesn't matter much. It's over now.

    Listen, this is so incredible you might not believe it happened. I do because it did, but I think it seems more real and horrifying to the two little daughters of the lady, one of my saviors, who loaned me the typewriter. To me, it simply happened.

    The American consulate is checking my identity and will get me another passport. I have six hundred dollars left in Denver. Lost three hundred in the river. I don't know what this hospital is going to cost. Some kind people have offered to help. The Shell lady says I can come to their house when I get out of here. I don't have any plans yet. Maybe I can write a story about this.

    All my best,
    Jack

Harbin

In September of 1986 the director of UCSF's laboratory animal facility invited me to accompany him to China to advise on a new animal care facility for at the Harbin Veterinary Research Institute. Joe and a veterinarian from Penn had been there the year before to kick off conceptual and schematic design, and the Chinese wanted them to review the results and help move into detailed design. Joe told them they needed an architect and mechanical engineer more than they needed him. They insisted that he come and said they had an architect but asked if he could find an engineer. Our work would be pro bono, but they would cover expenses for us and our wives for a week in Harbin working and a week afterwards visiting Beijing. UCSF generously gave us paid leave for the two weeks.

Joe and his wife Ella, Bill from Penn, and my wife Mary and I were met at the Beijing airport at midnight by five people: a Dr Zhang from the HVRI, a Ms Hu and another man from the Ministry of Agriculture, and an interpreter and her husband. Our coming was clearly important.

On the forty-five minute drive to town, a moped zipped out of the darkness to cross the highway. Our driver slammed on the brakes, the car skidded wildly and missed it by no more than a foot—and both parties simply continued on. No honking, fist-waving or recrimination, not even a mutter from our driver. Further on a group of people stood by the side of the road. There must have been an accident, we thought, given the way people were driving. Nope: Something was being cooked over a fire in a brazier.

    Then came an astounding number of pools of light containing construction sites. Over the following days we saw that a generic 15-story apartment building was being replicated everywhere using fairly unskilled labor. Once a reinforced concrete floor was poured from wooden scaffolding, the scaffolding was raised to pour the next. Nets just above the ground caught, presumably, falling material and workers. Our companions told us the apartments were much sought after for their private bathrooms, gas stoves, and elevators.

    We slept at the Friendship Hotel. It was reassuring to find smoke detectors throughout and fire extinguishers and hose cabinets in the corridors. In each room were a thermos of boiled water, two porcelain cups with lids, two packets of jasmine tea, and under the bed two pairs of paper slippers.

    Cicadas clattered all night and the next hot and sultry morning. Many plants were familiar: weeping willow, birch, maple, six story tall trees like cottonwoods that rose twenty feet before branching, other trees with broad two-lobed light green leaves edged in cream. Shrubbery was juniper and box hedge. A mosquito that bit me didn't seem particularly foreign, either.

    The taxis were Toyota Crowns; in fact, most of the automobiles were Japanese, though there were a Mercedes, a Ford van, and a Russian sedan parked outside. The trucks were Chinese and resembled two-ton Dodges from the fifties. No seatbelts. International style traffic signage.

    We flew to Harbin with Dr Zhang and Ms Hu. Six or seven people met us at the airport including the deputy director of the HVRI, Mr Chen Yukun, and four translators. A Ms Yang would accompany Mary and Ella on a trip to Jingpo Lake later in the week. A Mr Chen Bin Ri headed the Institute's translation department and had recently returned from Zaire after four years. Mary and I were delighted to find that he spoke French and tickled because we had met while working in San Francisco on a project being built in Zaire.

We rode into town with translator Chen Jiaqi, who had learned English by himself during the Cultural Revolution. During the eight years that the schools were closed, Chairman Mao had sent the students, teachers and intellectuals to experience the peasant basis of China's economy by working in the fields. Chen's vocabulary wasn't bad, but his pronunciation (like many others') was hard to understand.

The highway passed through two villages with houses of daubed clay brick and thatched roofs. The primitive buildings and meandering dirt tracks reminded me of a South Dakota Indian reservation where I'd lived as a child. Small tractors, donkeys, and horses pulled carts. Two-animal teams were invariably a donkey and a horse, though I saw one wagon pulled by three horses.

People were everywhere—walking, riding bicycles, riding in carts, working in the fields. Not a single person was idle. Everyone was working or going somewhere. In other countries, people lounge around alongside the road and talk or sleep. Here everyone moved. And they all seemed to be in good health: no disfigurations, no diseased eyes, no mutilations.

As we approached Harbin, the buildings were fired brick. It seems that on the western outskirts the peasants used it for new houses; elsewhere they used concrete. Some architecture, especially older buildings, showed European influence, undoubtedly Russian. Harbin had been an important stop on the Trans-Siberian Railway; in fact, we later met an old White Russian woman who had come after the revolution.

After a flat tire and passenger reshuffle we arrived at the Peace Hotel. The roomy rooms had an American-style bath and shower (though no hot water this afternoon), a lavatory (though ours was missing a drain plug), carpeted floor, comfortable beds, a thermos of hot water on the table, and a small refrigerator with a bottle of beer and a can of salted peanuts. Later two bottles of orange soda appeared. Funny, both here and at the Friendship Hotel there were thermometers instead of thermostats—you knew the temperature but could not control it. Each exterior opening had two complete sets of doors or windows; evidently double-glazed assemblies hadn't made it to Harbin. An old Russian-looking building next door for Chinese patrons was once the home of the provincial governor. It was rather shabby and had several cots in each room.

Joe, Bill and I caucused briefly to discuss goals for our first meeting. They had some small changes to the room layout to propose and I wanted to discuss the winter outside design temperature. I thought it should probably be minus 40 C instead of the minus 29 that was being used.

HVRI director Dr Ma Siqi arrived with interpreters Mr Yang and francophone Mr Chen. Dr Ma was a gentle man whose eyes ran constantly, which Joe told me later was due to something that had happened during the Cultural Revolution. Dr Ma said we could raise our issues at tomorrow's kickoff meeting.

Then we banqueted. Given that it was Saturday, I was surprised at the turnout. Among them were several people I would be working with: Engineer Liu Zhong Yu of the Heilongjiang Association of Heating Ventilating and Air Conditioning section of the Harbin Construction Designing Institute, Architect Gao Qunru of the Harbin Institute of Architectural Design, four engineers from the Institute of Air Conditioning at the China Academy of Building Research in Beijing, two controls engineers from the Harbin Institute of Architectural Design, an engineer employed by the Ministry of Agriculture to monitor proceedings, the construction manager, a representative from the local Communist party, and several others. It took days to figure out who was who.

Communication was patchy but everyone was cheerful and welcoming, and the food was interesting. Among other things we had small bumpy slugs called sea cucumbers and a delicious wild grouse called Paradise Bird.

Afterwards the five of us took a long walk. As on all our walks, Joe talked to everyone, took their pictures, and handed out balloons he blew up for children. We went through crowded streets to a place he called the night market. It was 9:30 and only a few food stalls selling roast chickens (for less than a dollar) were still open, not that we were hungry. An English-speaking industrial engineering student joined us on the walk back.

Mary and I had expected China to be similar to San Francisco's Chinatown though novel in the way of foreign places, but we were often surprised. The smells, for instance, were very intense. Here and there was sewage and elsewhere odors we couldn't identify.

I stood on the balcony of our hotel room looking into the street before the Sunday sun was quite up. In each direction were a sidewalk, divider, bike lane, another divider, and two vehicle lanes. Electric trolleys ran on tracks; there were many buses, some diesel, some electric; and a multitude of bicycles, often carrying two people and even three: a child on the handlebars, a man pedaling, and a woman sidesaddle behind. Six or seven young men in jogging suits trotted along.

In the afternoon Joe, Bill and I were driven to the Institute to meet with the whole project group. Dr Chen presented a list of forty-three questions that he hoped we could help them answer. That took quite a while and we only had time to say that we had a couple things to discuss too but would hold them for later.

After a hurried dinner we went to the opera, which started at 6:00, like last evening's banquet. People sat in chairs or on the floor. They ate and spat and smoked cigarettes and talked constantly. Now and then, usually after what seemed to have been an aria, there would be a short, intense burst of applause followed by noisy discussion which reverberated within the plaster walls.

Costumes were ornate and makeup was showy and intricate. The women all had red eyes. The warrior prince protagonist wore a hoop as a symbol of authority and five-foot long pheasant feathers on the sides of his head like ram horns as a symbol of power. The fourth son of the Yang family, he had been kidnapped by a neighboring province and then married the princess. They had a child. The princess's mother became empress when her husband died.

The story begins. His wife sees that he is sad and begins guessing why: My mother has been mean to you? No, no. You've been plying your tool with another woman? No, you're wrong. I'm so discourteous, she says, I can't guess. Are you displeased with our house and would rather live in the palace we visited yesterday? No, that's not it. Please excuse me for being discourteous and not guessing. More about courtesy and their lack of frankness with each other—for example, the prince has never told her his name. Finally it emerges that he's homesick. Oh my god, she says, that's terrible! He would like to visit his mother, most of whose many sons have been killed in battle.

The princess goes to her mother the empress. In order for him to cross the border, he must carry a ceremonial sword to show the border guards as a passport since they have orders to not let anyone leave without it. She can't think of how to get the sword from her mother. Finally she pinches her child to make it cry. (The child is a dummy.) The empress asks why the child is crying and the daughter says it's because he wants to play with the sword. The empress says, well, ordinarily I don't give this sword out, but since you're my daughter and this is my grandson, I'll let you have it.

The princess gives it to her husband, who is very happy to get it. There is a condition, though—it must be returned the following morning. The husband quickly rides off with a companion. The actors swing three-foot long thongs with dangling threads to show they are riding horses. At the border are two guards dressed like clowns in domino—black and white costumes and white faces. The sword is shown and our hero passes.

The person in charge of the neighboring border is also wearing two fancy feathers. He is the son of the prince's younger brother, the fifth son. Or the sixth and our prince is the fifth—our interpreter wasn't sure. The nephew handcuffs the prince and takes him to his father. After a bit of discussion the brothers recognize each other, or our prince tells the other that they are brothers. They're very happy.

Intermission. The audience replenished food and drink.

The prince's mother enters and they recognize each other with much weeping expressed by touching their eyes with their elbows. The son bows and kowtows three times. (Everything in this opera happens in threes.) They talk. He tells her that he's been living in the neighboring country for fifteen years and has changed his name and taken a wife. The mother is unhappy about the name change but says, well, we can talk about that later. He says, well, I wish we could, but I have to go right back; my wife will be killed if the sword isn't returned. Much stylized crying and wailing and elbows to eyes. My heart is torn in half, he says—if I stay my wife gets killed, and if I leave you feel bad. Eventually his mother consents to his return. More weeping and wailing and then he leaves.

The guards at the border arrest him because they think there's something fishy about the sword. They take him in handcuffs to the empress who says, Off with his head. One of the guards goes to get the daughter. When she arrives the mother asks why she came. Daughter: To find out why my husband was arrested. Mother: You're asking me? You stole my sword and you're asking me? Off with your head, too. (By the way, earlier the empress had sung about how peace-loving she is; now she's executing her daughter and son-in-law.) Wailing and elbows to the eyes about how sorry they both are. The border clowns get up and ask for clemency for these two. The empress says off with their heads too. Now everybody's sad.

Guards to daughter: Why don't you beseech your mother, that'll take care of it. The daughter beseeches three times but it doesn't work. The guards think of a trick and tell her: Give your son to your mother and then pretend to kill yourself. Which she does, and the mother says, no, no, don't kill yourself, you're spared. Daughter: I'm sorry, I'm sorry, I'm sorry. The mother gives in, everyone is happy, everyone knows everyone else's name and that's the end.

One of our interpreters didn't care much for opera; he said it was for old people. Another knew something about it and seemed to have enjoyed this one.

As we waited for our ride to the Institute Monday morning, a woman rode by on a bicycle with a little boy carrying a turkey in a basket. The turkey's head poked up and looked around. A woman with a boy waiting for a bus smiled at Mary and gave her a wave when they were on. Not everyone managed to get on, though. People pushed and shoved, knocked over a woman, were even hanging off the doors as the bus left.

In general, people were friendly. They weren't pushy (to us!) and there was no undertone of violence or the resentment that you feel many places. They stared, but out of curiosity, not scorn or anger or envy because you have something they don't. Mary felt like she could leave her purse or camera anywhere and nobody would consider taking it, and she didn't worry about getting hit over the head in a dark alley.

There did seem to be class distinctions, but people talked to each other without signs of subservience. Most were clearly poor and uneducated, but maybe the distinctions of wealth and education were less pronounced than they'd been before the revolution. There had certainly been many simple people at the opera who enjoyed it immensely.

Joe, Bill and I finally aired our design concerns and reached some agreements. One was to raise the ceiling height in the animal cubicles from 2.5 to 3.1 meters. Another was that the winter outdoor design temperature would remain minus 29 C. The Chinese said it seldom dropped that low, and even more rarely to minus 40. Bill thought the animals could tolerate lowish room temperatures for short periods so Joe and I capitulated. We reached consensus on levels of air filtration, unit redundancy, and the inclusion of an ethylene glycol piping loop to transfer heat from the exhaust air to the outside (fresh) air stream. I began filling a notebook with decisions, questions, things to be done.

After lunch I met alone with the five engineers and began by asking how they were coming with load calculations. There was some confusion, partly due to interpreter Chen Jiaqi's poor language skills, and then it turned out that Mr Liu, the Harbin engineer, had planned a presentation to discuss his design so far. So we slowly and laboriously waded through the design conditions for winter and summer, indoor and outdoor, and so on and so forth. He wanted electric, not pneumatic, controls. He wanted a packaged air conditioning unit preassembled with controls shipped from the US so all they had to do was install it. I pointed out that there would be some field wiring, which he didn't seem to realize, and wondered to myself if they would be capable of it. The presentation took almost three hours. I had to teach Chen the English words for equipment, and the engineers had to teach him the Chinese. Engineer Liu finally finished by listing the things he wanted help with: specifying the filters, coils, fans, chillers, pumps, heat reclaim unit, and controls—in other words, everything except sizing the ductwork.

When he stopped, I said there were three things I wanted to discuss. One was the heat reclaim system. They got excited and talked about it at length among themselves and said they liked the idea; they hadn't thought about it. I was mildly surprised, since they had approved it in the general session that morning, but maybe they meant that they hadn't thought about it during their own design sessions. The second thing was the supply air temperature, which we agreed to discuss the next morning. The third was system design for redundancy, and I rapidly sketched my thoughts on paper. We would discuss them another time, too.

At the hotel in the evening I decided that we should first calculate new air quantities based on the higher ceiling, then figure out the needed static pressure, and then do a rough selection of fans, coils, filters and so on.

We were up early Tuesday because breakfast was to be served at six, but everything downstairs was dark and locked up, including the building doors. That made us wonder how we would get out if there was ever a fire, so we searched until we found a window that we could open.

Mary and Ella left for Jingpo Lake in a four-wheel drive Toyota Land Rover with Ms Hu from the China Academy of Sciences, Miss Zho from some institution in Harbin, Ms Yang their interpreter, and a driver. Someone else took the train to meet them there. Ms Hu stowed watermelon for a break on the ten-hour trip next to cans of gasoline in the back.

Joe, Bill and I were driven to the Institute. During our meetings we drank green tea from pretty lidded ceramic cups. The leaves sink to the bottom, and assistants continually replenished the water from thermos bottles. Engineer Liu smoked and so did the Institute's construction manager, an older man with glasses and bad teeth. Since the windows were open and the room was large and we were well spaced out on sofas and easy chairs, I did too.

Two young Harbin men, one of them Professor Zhang's son, were designing the controls with advice from a very nice white-haired gentleman from Beijing who had worked for Staefa in Switzerland. A short, heavyset man with an abrupt, sarcastic manner was a filter expert. A second filter expert from Beijing was sitting in the architectural design group with Joe and Bill. There was also a woman air conditioning expert from Beijing and the engineer from the Ministry of Agriculture about my age who everyone called their boss.

My sinuses were clogged and I was very tired, but I led the calculations of air quantities and static pressure so we could select equipment in the afternoon. We discussed the design procedure. Harbin and Beijing would review the design among themselves and send the completed drawings, specifications, and equipment lists to me for review. If I had extensive comments, they would make changes and send me everything for a final review. I would send it on to Dr Hsu, Bill's boss at Penn. Dr Hsu had gone to school with the Minister of Agriculture and had the final say on the design.

At lunch I learned that the Beijing controls engineer was returning that night, so I suggested that we put off equipment selection and talk about controls instead.

The controls scheme worked up by Professor Zhang's son was very good; I only suggested relocating a couple sensors and controlling steam pressure differently. His scheme had a thermostat and a temperature sensor in each room. The sensor reported to a central panel that did the controlling, and if the panel went down it could be bypassed and the thermostat would control. Me, I thought it would be better to control from the thermostat and only use the panel to monitor, so that in an emergency they wouldn't have the worry of bypassing it, but I couldn't convince them. I dropped it. Persuasion, concession and consensus move a project along, and it was good to remember hearing an architect say that four engineers discussing controls will come up with six schemes each of which is unassailably the best.

We talked for a long time about room air pressure control. The pathogens that would be studied in the rooms were very dangerous and their isolation was critical. The Beijing filter man wanted to average the pressure differentials between several zones to control discharge dampers at the supply fans. It sounded like a good idea, but we found some situations where it would give bad results and finally settled on placing pressure sensors at the air handlers, in the spaces, and outside the building. Exhaust fan dampers would modulate to keep space pressure negative with respect to outside.

Back at the hotel, the electrical circuit that served the refrigerator and television had blown a fuse. A young guy who spoke good English came with a screwdriver and opened the fuse box. The fuses were big ceramic blocks three inches long by an inch wide. He found the bad one and started unscrewing something. When I leaned over curiously he backed up, not wanting me to see. When I said I was an engineer, he said oh, okay, and showed me. The ceramic block had two screws between which was a thin piece of wire. He replaced the wire and everything worked again.

We talked for a while about what he did and what I did and then he surprised me by asking if I'd like to go dancing.

I went next door and asked Bill if he was interested. The guy told us that a couple blocks down the street by the river was a building with a cantilevered second floor where the ballroom was.

Bill and I walked over and saw through the windows many people sitting on sofas. Those dancing held each other a foot apart for both slow and fast dances as they rotated and revolved around the room like we did in grade school. We were too bashful to go in.

Instead we walked on and watched people mix concrete for a new building. An odd noise led us to men shoveling gravel from the back of dump trucks into two-wheeled carts. The people with the carts got a running start up a slight incline to dump the gravel into a hopper where cement and sand were added. The hopper was lifted by two ropes and dumped into a mixer where water was added. On the other side of the mixer a lineup of people with more carts waited to take the concrete away. It was just like the lineups of diesel-powered machinery you see in the US, merely different technology.

There was construction everywhere late into the night and materials everywhere in the streets. Two- and three-story buildings were brick, even one five-story building; the rest were concrete. Some sites had cranes and some didn't. Some cranes moved alongside the building on rails. I never saw how they got materials up without one.

Harbin was pretty, foliage and flowers everywhere, though winters must be mighty gray and brown. Streets were asphalt, cobblestone, and dirt. It was very dusty and coal smoke was pervasive; our nostrils were black by evening every day, and I finally realized that the tea cosy on the television set in my hotel room was for dust protection.

Wednesday morning we continued to design pressure control and select the steam piping. At lunch we learned that the architectural group had raised the ceilings some more, so we would have to recalculate air quantities.

During the afternoon we worked out the dimensions of

the air handling units. I said the filters would be the same size as the coils because they were based on 500 feet per minute face velocity. The Beijing filter guy with glasses said no, the HEPAs don't run that high. I checked the catalogue; he was right. Live and learn. Onward to fans, coils, humidifier, piping, frames, plenums, dampers, installation details.

I told them that we should copy our equipment layout from the blackboard onto a sheet of paper and label each component. Then we would use the same labels on the equipment schedule so that you could look from the schedule to the drawing and see what went where. They thought that was a grand idea and I realized that besides engineering and sharing my knowledge, I was showing them how to put together purchasing and construction documents. I wondered if they would have time to produce a book of specifications. Dr Hsu wanted us to list the model numbers of three different manufacturers but we would not have enough time together to do it. I doubted that we'd be able to finish for even one manufacturer, but I thought they were learning enough to complete it by themselves. Mr Liu would try to complete it and then meet with the Beijing engineers.

I discovered that the Institute repaired refrigerators for supplemental income so I selected a type of chiller that uses reciprocating rather than centrifugal compressors. (A chiller is a giant refrigerator that chills water which circulates in coils like automobile radiators to cool the air that is supplied to the rooms. The chiller itself is cooled by air drawn across its refrigerant coils by fans that blow the now hot air upwards.) This type of chiller is placed outdoors, as it needs a lot of air to operate.

The engineers and architects and managers were worried that the chillers would freeze in the cold Harbin winters. I assured them that they were used in the equally cold northern Great Plains without problem, but they were so worried that I promised I would get a letter from the manufacturer saying they would work fine.

That night was clear and beautiful with a cool breeze,

gibbous moon and stars everywhere. The street was full of foot, bike, bus and car traffic. I spent the evening making up blank schedules that showed what needed to be done for the rest of the equipment.

    Thursday we concentrated on calculations and equipment selections and layout.
    In the evening Mary and Ella returned from Jingpo Lake. They'd eaten a lot of fish heads, rice and melons, and Mary was sick of food and too tired to go with us to Chen Yukun's house for dinner. Too bad—it was extraordinary!
    Chen's wife and daughter-in-law cooked many dishes in a tiny kitchen: Chicken prepared two ways and served on the same plate, rabbit prepared three, dragon fish cut along the spine with the two sides spread in coils on each side of the head. Sea cucumber, a shrimp dish, a pork dish. Bread baked earlier in the day (rice is not eaten in the northeast). Each was delicious, and dessert was stunning! You picked up a piece of potato and doused it in a pot of molten sugar, then dipped it, trailing a long string of caramel, into a bowl of cold water just long enough that it wouldn't burn your mouth, and popped it in. Exquisite. And then another round with apples. Drinks were port wine, beer and mao tai, a spirit made from sorghum. I was looped when we left.

    Friday was recreational. The entire project team took an excursion on the Songhua River where we cruised up and down under the old steel railroad bridge and the new concrete auto bridge and then to Sun Island. Chen Yukun paid for entrance tickets to the small park and we strolled to a building cantilevered over a pretty lake, looked at a rocky man-made island with the Chinese-style bridges we had expected to see but hadn't until now, took pictures of each other, had Mary's silhouette drawn by an artist on the path.
    Back at the boat they asked if we would like lunch inside or outside. We said outside in the fresh air, so they started fooling around with a table and then said, oh, why don't you

all go down and rest inside. So we went down and saw a table already laid and thought, well, this isn't so bad, and asked interpreter Yang if they had sent us down so we would decide that it would be better to have lunch there. He said yes so we said well then, tell them we'll have it inside. There were canned sardines in tomato sauce, cold chicken, hard-boiled eggs black inside with dark yellow yolks called *pidan,* thousand-year egg, and *cha jir dai,* eggs hard-boiled in tea. Those were pretty good, but the pidan had a peculiar aftertaste and rubbery texture, especially the outside quarter inch. While we ate the boat returned to dock.

This part of town near the river was the older commercial center, with cobblestone and asphalt streets and many trees. The buildings were better built than those near our hotel and the Institute.

We walked to a nearby bird and flower market that had exactly two parakeets and a couple tanks of goldfish for sale, and not many plants, either—four roses, a few rubber plants, two or three geraniums. How could they make a living?

Beneath a billboard advertising the Harbin Comprehensive Dairy was a department store where Mary had been with Ellen and bought a typically Chinese thermos for her sister. They'd been quite taken with the smell of gasoline as you went upstairs. My great-grandfather's pocket watch had just stopped working so we went to look at wristwatches on the fourth floor, where the smell of gasoline was indeed impressive. I bought a wristwatch made locally for nine dollars but it only lasted a couple years.

We hopped into cars and headed for the Northeast Agricultural Academy, from which Professor Zhang had graduated. The academy had moved from downtown to the countryside when Chairman Mao said agricultural schools should be in the country. Professor Zhang very much wanted Joe and Bill to visit and was concerned that we wouldn't get across the railroad tracks in front before the trains started switching, because the wait could be as long as an hour. Alas, we got there just as they began.

One of the drivers thought he knew how to go around them. We drove onto a very bumpy road and on and on to another road off to the right but the other driver said no, that's not the way, so we kept going very slowly through huge potholes and so much dust that we had to close the windows. I had to close my eyes to keep it from my contacts.

The next road was impassible because of construction, so we turned around and went back to the first. It filled with vehicles and dust as we bounced through fields as far as we could see on one side and on the other the brick wall that surrounded the academy. We went on and on and on, took a turn that turned out to be a dead end, went back. I began to think that even the locals giving us directions didn't know how to get to the academy from there, though we were circling it and could often see a modern nine-story building.

At last we got back to the main road on the other side of the tracks, but it was impassible because of construction. The detour was a very narrow, bumpy, dusty road between walls just feet from each side and then, around a corner, was a half-overturned truck blocking the road. We got out and looked at the truck and looked at the locals with their dirty faces and clothes and they looked at us, and finally the drivers decided to try to get around the truck. While they somehow they managed that, we walked a short way through a small, incredibly dirty village. I felt we were in a movie about some primitive, filthy place. And yet, two little girls dressed in clean, pink jackets ran up to stare at us as we got back in the cars. Then another road and down a dead end, backtracked and took another, and finally got to the academy two hours late.

The dean of the school of veterinary medicine spoke good English and took us in a businesslike but somewhat rushed manner through a microbiology room, classroom, sample room, specimen room, and then the large animal clinic. We looked around the bare concrete room as he pointed to this and that and then to some equipment and said, these are the lasers that we use for anesthesia. Joe and Bill didn't understand and asked what was used for anesthesia. The dean said, these lasers. Lasers? Carbon dioxide and helium. How do you use carbon dioxide and helium for anesthesia? These are carbon dioxide and helium lasers, I said. Bill, ordinarily phlegmatic, grew very excited when he caught on. The dean explained that they aim the lasers for thirty minutes at two points on the animal, although one is sufficient, to produce a general anesthesia that lasts one or two hours. If necessary they can do it again. Bill asked so many questions that the dean called in the anesthesiologist to answer. I think it was the high point of Bill's trip.

Somewhere else a fellow was directing a laser at a pig's vagina in an experiment to stimulate hormone production. Her squeals drove Ella and Mary away.

After dinner back at the hotel we went for a walk. The dust and smoke in the air were so thick it looked like San Francisco on a foggy day. The streets we took were unpaved and rutted. It felt like London of two hundred years ago, the same squalor and garbage and open sewers. Joe commented that humanity's greatest advance in hygiene was putting sewers underground. Ella said China reminded them of the US thirty years ago what with the old-fashioned car styles and antimacassars on furniture. Well, China was quite a mix—primitive filth and hyperbolic cooling towers, donkey carts and diesel engines, acupuncture and laser anesthesia, this specific pathogen free animal facility we were designing.

Ma, Chen, Joe, Bill and I toured the Institute Saturday morning and then developed a schedule of tasks, responsibilities, and target dates for moving forward. After lunch, the entire group went over the list of questions we had begun with last Sunday. We were satisfied with the progress we had made. They agreed to a final suggestion of mine to include one of the chillers and air handlers in the emergency power coverage already planned for the controls and fire alarm systems so that at least some of the animals wouldn't die if they lost normal power. When the meeting ended, we were finished. I had worked some fifty-five hours that week.

The Institute people came to the hotel Sunday morning to say goodbye. Professor Zhang took me aside and very tactfully asked if I could arrange for his son to move to the United States, perhaps by finding him a training program in controls. I said I didn't know of programs like that but would see what I could do. At home, I found that there was indeed no such thing—people learn on the job, and it was impossible to get him a job given his lack of experience and visa. Joe, on the other hand, was able to offer an internship in his own department to a veterinarian he'd been working with; the young man and his wife eventually became citizens.

I had forgotten until we reached the metal detector and machine gun-armed guards in the airport that I hadn't packed my pocketknife in my suitcase. Goodbye pocketknife, I thought as I gave it up. But hooray! As the plane descended over the Great Wall into Beijing, a stewardess presented it to me on a tray. And instead of taking a pilot hostage I merely thanked her.

The Ministry of Agriculture took over hosting us beginning with a banquet that evening.

The next day Mary, Bill, interpreter Chen Jiaqi and I went to the Great Wall at Mutianyu and obeyed the signs.

NO SMOKING ON THE MOUNTAIN DONT TUSE OPEN OPEN FIRE

CARVING AND SCRIBBLING NOT ALLOWED ON THE WALL UNDER PENALTY OF A FIRE

SMOKING AND LIGHTING IS PROHIBITED ON THE HILL UNDER PENDITY OF A FIRE

YOU BE A TRUE HERO WELCOME TO TAKE THE CABLEWAY

We walked, though, and after the wall we visited the Ming Tombs.

Back at the hotel, a terrible place in a pleasant park near the Friendship Hotel, we had a horrible dinner of sea cucumbers. I never cared for their sweet taste or texture of snot-covered sponge, though some places did prepare them better than others. Because they were a delicacy they were offered every lunch and dinner.

In the mornings old men with caged birds sat in the park. One day a man played a two-stringed violin, an *erhu*, while another sang. Old people did tai chi in groups and there were many swimmers in the lake.

Joe and Bill met at the Ministry Tuesday morning. In the afternoon we all visited the Summer Palace. That evening we went to an opera in a small theater.

It was lighter and funnier than the one we'd seen in Harbin. A dragon woman and her friend fly over a village suffering from drought and see two attractive young men. The women bring rain from the clouds, descend to the village and fall in love with the young men. They want to get married but the dragon woman's father says no—another young man, a dragon dressed in black, wants to marry her. This suitor is quite jealous and punishes her by removing her scales so that she becomes mortal.

After intermission the young village man and his sidekick have gone to the emperor's palace with a small memento that the dragon woman had given him. There he meets a high official, a minister, whose wife is ill. The memento cures the wife and the minister rewards the young man by taking him on as secretary. Eventually he becomes a deputy minister.

Now, it seems that the minister has also adopted the dragon woman and her friend. The minister wants to marry his adopted daughters to his deputy and village friend, but because the men don't recognize the women, they say they cannot marry since they're in love with others. The women favor the marriage because they've recognized the men. The dragon woman is brought in wearing a veil and the young man is dragged out screaming.

The marriage takes place offstage. The last scene has us in the newlyweds' bedchamber where the man is supposed to take the veil off to consummate the marriage, but he refuses. Eventually she takes it off herself. He shrieks and sings and finally looks at her, recognizes her, and all ends happily.

The curtains closed and Ms Hu's young assistant took us onto the stage to meet the sweaty and exhausted but welcoming cast. We said how wonderful it had been and the young man who played the young man said thank you, thank you in English.

A Ms Wang of Beijing University came for breakfast Wednesday. Apparently she had introduced the turkey to China as George Washington Carver the peanut to the US. She gave us a turkey cookbook she had compiled, but unfortunately we never could use it; it was in Chinese.

She took Joe and Bill somewhere for the morning. Mary, Ella, and I went to a street of antique shops that sold old silk embroideries, modern lithographs, sheet music for piano, taped folk and popular music.

At noon we met at the Fragrant Hills Hotel for a banquet with the president of the university and two or three deans. Then Joe, Bill and I went with Ms Wang and a dean to the university where we talked all afternoon about her plans to set up a laboratory affiliated with the Ministry that would test research done at institutes around the country and also adjudicate between them if they developed different cures for a disease. Bill understood it to be something like the FDA.

Joe had complained to someone about our hotel and bad food. That evening we were taken to the Friendship Hotel for dinner and the next morning we moved to the Beijing Vegetable Research Institute's countryside guest house, a lovely set of bungalows near a pond. Then back into town for shopping at a place the drivers knew of, not the Friendship Store for a change, where we bought a small rug that would fit into our suitcases and an embroidered dragon. Lunch at the Friendship Hotel. We liked the signs there.

> WILD GAME IS SERVED HERE

> THE BARBECUE SCHEDULED FOR SEPT 20 AT 7 PM HAS BEEN CANCELLED FOR SOME REASONS

We liked the billboards around town, too.

> BEIJING GOLF CLUB: PECULIAR DESIGN

> A BID FOR THE OLYMPICS QUICKENS OUR MARCH TOWARD 2000

> IF YOU DRINK BEIGUO BEER, IT WILL MAKE YOU FEEL TASTY

> REGAIN YOUR VIGOUR IN TOURISM

We vigorously toured Tiananmen Square and the Forbidden City, then Tiantan (the Temple of Heaven) with its Echo Wall which the guides, like guides everywhere there is such a thing, pressed us to try for ourselves.

I finally took a close look at the bicycles. They're one-speed, with hand brakes. The front brake is below the handlebar like ours, but the rear brake is low on the back post near the sprocket. Where our rear brake is found, at the top of the post, is a lock with pinchers that go through the wheel.

We went to the Friendship Hotel for dinner but when we arrived Ms Hu's assistant told us there had been a change in plans because the restaurant couldn't make the caramelized dessert. Instead we banqueted at a very fancy place with Ms Hu and the vice president of the foreign affairs branch of the Ministry of Agriculture, a funny guy full of jokes who had spent four years in Italy as the Chinese representative for something or other. He told us that Italians and Americans were fairly informal, but oh, the English!, and imitated their stiff propriety. Dessert was made with lychee this time. Moon cakes followed since it was the mid-autumn festival.

Back at the guest house a young man who spoke some English invited us to join the staff later when they were going to sing and dance. We didn't stay up that late but did walk by the pond and eat more moon cakes with the director of the Institute and her husband, a veterinarian from a nearby institute who happened to know CK Hsu, and four younger people who chatted and gazed at the moon.

On the flight home I talked with a fellow returning to North Carolina after two weeks in Qingdao where he had helped start up a plastic injection molding plant. The Chinese bought toy molds at scrap prices from American companies whose products had gone out of style. Another fellow who worked for a drilling company thirty-five days on and thirty-five off was headed home to Oklahoma for his off-time. We had all been surprised at how elementary Chinese technology was but we'd all found that they badly wanted to learn, worked hard, and were very hospitable.

The Beijing engineers knew their craft, but I thought they had benefitted from hearing about other design techniques. Engineer Liu had been floundering around, not knowing even how to begin, but we had spelled out the next steps. I hoped he could carry on.

The chiller manufacturer's rep laughed when I asked for a letter confirming that the equipment would operate in Harbin's winter, but he had the factory write one, which I forwarded to China.

Eight months later, in May of 1987, I wrote to an engineer friend:
The China project is creeping along. The mechanical engineer is utterly lacking in HVAC experience, which isn't necessarily a show-stopper, but he is also stupid, lazy, obtuse, and

resistant to change. Last September I spent a week in Harbin with him and seven other engineers to design the system but saw at once that we would not have time, so I showed them how to design it, and we agreed on who would do what. Liu was to do the load calcs (simple because it's 100% outside air and exhaust) and send the design conditions to me so I could check his calcs and pass the results on to Carrier and Trane for equipment selection, and send the selections back to him who in the meantime would have designed the ductwork and machine room. He would check the equipment against the preliminary selections we did in Harbin, make minor adjustments to the layout if needed, send the design to me for review and comment, incorporate my comments, and that would be that.

In November, having received nothing, I sent a letter asking if they were stuck on something, and again hearing nothing, I sent a list summarizing the design criteria we needed. In January, Liu returned my list with some information filled in, some missing, and much that was unnecessary. He also wrote that he had sent a big package.

In February, a young veterinarian from Harbin came to train at UCSF's animal care facility and brought a question from his boss: What is Engineer Dr Oakley doing?—we haven't heard anything from him. I told him I was waiting for Liu's package and hoping that it would have the design calcs. He telephoned his boss, who airmailed me a copy which arrived the beginning of March. Liu's package finally arrived in April, as he had sent it by surface mail.

It was dismaying. Some of the calcs were indecipherable. The ones I could follow had so many errors that I had no confidence in the results. The psych charts were incomplete. He had changed the zone pressures that we had agreed on in September. So I did the blasted calculations myself and contacted Trane, who didn't show much interest, and Carrier, whose International Division got working on it. Then their guy retired, which I found out last week when I talked to his successor, but at least he finished it up right away.

This has been frustrating. I said twice during the meetings that they should be sure to post mail by air because surface mail could take months. This simple, repeated instruction was not followed by my friend Mr Liu; what chance is there that more complicated instructions will be followed? At one point I quizzed him about why his duct design showed three main trunks the same size for the entire length of the building. He answered that it made balancing easier and continued with a confusing disquisition on velocity, air quantity, duct area and pressure. I replied by going back to basics: $Q=VA$. As the air quantity drops, so does its velocity (and pressure) unless you make the duct smaller. The Beijing engineers followed perfectly—I was embarrassed thinking that I might insult them by trotting out such basic concepts—in fact, even the non-engineers in the room followed. Liu was either too stupid to understand or saw that he had erred but was loath to admit it. He insisted that the pressure in the duct would be the same everywhere if the shape was constant. Then it occurred to me to ask how they sized ductwork and transitions—did they use formulas and graphs? Yes. The light dawned. No wonder he hadn't changed sizes: The formula and graph method is so tedious that he had probably been avoiding it since he met it in school. Now he'd forgotten how, was afraid to try, and had come up with this nonsense as justification. Well, I snatched my Ductulator [Trane's simple tool with a cardboard wheel marked with air velocity and pressure loss that rotates against another piece marked with air quantity and duct size] and said, here, look at this! magic! and showed him how to size ductwork. He sat in a corner for ten minutes playing with it and when I left I gave it to him. But when his package arrived, it included a request that I design the ductwork, as he didn't know how.

Beyond Liu's balkiness, there is a more serious problem. All the people we worked with except maybe Liu listened hard and were keen to learn. But my veterinarian colleagues and I often found ourselves in the middle of a discussion with the sinking and then sunk feeling that a point had not been understood. There is a huge amount of experience that we and the Chinese don't have in common. Not, of course, human qualities; I loved the people I met. They are kind and witty, thoughtful and friendly. People in the streets would look at us curiously and if we met their eye they would smile and nod or discreetly look away and then back with a smile. They are gentle and polite. Strangers did not fall over themselves to be at our service and some were grumpy or indifferent or busy as people everywhere are, but not once in two weeks did we experience hostility. I've never been anywhere like it.

But in the area of machines, we have different backgrounds. You and I grew up falling asleep in the back seat of cars; the vibration of machines is as familiar as our own body's. Consider that in the US there is one car for every three people whereas in the PRC it's one for 10,000. A young Englishman once surprised me with his snobbish pride at having a driver's license—at age twenty-three! He probably didn't know that we learned to drive on our fathers' knees at eleven. But how incomparably closer to ours is his experience than the Chinese. I don't think a single person among the engineers, doctors, veterinarians, directors and deans we met knows how to drive. The research institute employed three drivers to take them around. Now consider the rest of our machine culture, the knowledge in our bones that a billion Chinese don't have, and imagine the possibilities for miscommunication.

In October Joe and Ella, Bill and I went to Beijing to review the design at the Ministry of Agriculture.

Jet lag disorients me—I forget things, can't remember them for more than a few seconds, remember that there was something to do but not what, can't hold more than one thing in mind, although my concentration on that one thing is okay. I have lapses of self-confidence. One was occasioned by concern that I wasn't properly modulating a display of emotion to get an idea across.

The outcome of engineering, like anything involving people, is partly determined by how well you communicate.

Even in your native language you must monitor verbal and facial expressions, both your own and your interlocutor's, and phrase your thoughts with care. It's trickier when you talk through an interpreter who you're not sure understood what you meant in the first place and as to whose nuances of phrasing you have no clue.

Since the emergency generator would be inside the building, I'd told them last year to ask the manufacturer how much combustion and cooling air would be needed so they could size an intake wall louver and ductwork from the radiator to an exhaust louver. Now, with the group, I didn't find these things in the design. I asked neutrally why there were no louvers in the generator room. They said that because they didn't want to heat the cold winter air, and very cold it was, they had decided to have no openings in the walls. I was mildly amused but felt I had to convey the importance of getting air in and out, so I put on a display of dismay, then feared that it would be interpreted as sneering or scorn, was stricken with the desire to not imply that the designer had screwed up so badly that it was risible (although it was!), then couldn't judge the effect I was having and was suddenly unmoored from my bearings and shut up.

I hoped I was getting some ideas across and thankful that at least I managed to stay awake and function on roughly five hours of sleep. Unable to extract a whit of meaning from the spoken language, it became little more than one sound among others: birds chirping, susurrus of wind through the leaves, horns, truck exhaust, the swish and rumble of tires, dull distant explosions near the Great Wall. Taste and smell were also vivid, though that could have been due to the novel flavors and scents. Ice cream was more than usually refreshing.

The people were as much fun as ever. Interpreter Chen Jiaqi, two HVRI women and I crossed paths in the hotel corridor one day with an attractive young woman attending a convention of models who stared fixedly over the tops of our heads. I tapped one of the Harbin women on the shoulder and rolled my eyes. No, no, she said and drew herself back to look down her nose. We shared a pleasant laugh.

Evenings and one or two afternoons off we kept busy: another spot on the Great Wall; the zoo, where ordinary domestic dogs were exhibited; the Friendship Store again; an acrobatics performance; a revue that included a classical pianist, an army chorus, slapstick acts, and a short musical in which a young village wife in a group of women on one side of the stage sang goodbye to her husband on the other side in a group of men who had been drafted into the army. So that he could embrace their child one last time, she threw it in a long arc across the stage. Thank god he caught it! (Though it was only a doll.) I almost laughed aloud but the audience was somber and tears ran down Chen's cheeks.

Joe and Ella stayed in Beijing for five days of sightseeing, Bill took a train to southern China, and I flew to Shanghai. While Chen and I waited at the airport there for our driver, I lit a cigarette. A short, scowling, uniformed old lady pointed to a no smoking sign in Chinese on the back of a column and wrote me a citation. Times were a-changing. I put out the cigarette and paid the fine.

Chen was a simple fellow who wanted to please. His English was not great and his understanding was slow, but he didn't deserve to be treated like a bumpkin with a funny accent from the northern countryside by our driver. I told Chen to ignore him, but he said it wasn't as easy as all that because he barely understood the Shanghai dialect.

The driver liked to take me shopping because he took a small cut whenever he exchanged my dollars for yuan. One afternoon I said I wanted to go the old natural history museum mentioned in my guidebook so I could take pictures of the mummies to show my son.

"There's no such place," said the driver. "I'll take you to the Friendship Store."

"There is. Look here." And I showed him the address in the guidebook.

"Oh, that place. It's closed now."

"It should be open this time of day."

"No, it closed last winter."

"Let's just drive by and see."

"I'll take you to the Friendship Store."

I insisted. He finally capitulated and drove to a glass and steel building that looked like a convention center. "This doesn't look like a museum," I said.

"It is, it is."

I walked in to find a trade show of Dutch heavy construction equipment. I strode out with Chen and the driver following. "Take me to the natural history museum."

"It's closed."

"Fuck you," I said and took my backpack from the car and headed down the street much relieved to be away from him—though I suddenly realized I couldn't talk to anyone on my own.

"Dr Engineer Oakley! Dr Engineer Oakley!" Chen ran up. "You did the right thing!" he panted.

"Thanks," I said. "Now, have a look at this map. Where are we?"

It turned out that he didn't know how to read a map. I showed him what a street looked like but it was beyond him, so I pointed at a nearby street sign. "Okay, what does that say?"

He told me, I found its transliteration on the map, and there we were. "Follow me," I said, and led him to the museum. The mummies were disappointing shriveled up brown things, but I took a picture anyway.

The next day we drove sixty miles to visit the Grand Canal and the serene gardens in the bustling city of Suzhou. On the way back our driver stopped at a roadhouse in the middle of nowhere and ordered a huge mound of eel. It was delicious but so rich that Chen and I barely made a dent. The driver ate the rest with gusto.

Chen and I took the train to Hangzhou where we stayed two nights, saw temples and Buddhas and huge millipedes in the park across the lake, ate the famous roast chicken, and visited the Tea Research Institute south of town. It was always a treat to be shown around places like that by the people who work there, and it was generous of them since I had nothing to do with their work.

Two and a half years passed. A group of Chinese veterinarians, architects, and engineers visited UCSF and we met for a morning in my conference room. I was sorry I couldn't offer them the level of hospitality they had shown me but I was low on the totem pole at home. For lunch we went to a Chinese restaurant, of all things, and they went on to Philadelphia to visit Bill and CK Hsu.

Two more years later, in May 1992, Joe and Ella, Bill and I went to the opening ceremony. A night at the Friendship Hotel in Beijing, on to Harbin and the good old Peace Hotel the next day, and then a tour of the new building.

It was well built. The quality was good. But above the second floor, where we should have been on the roof, was a walled enclosure with big, irregular holes in a second roof. "What is this?" I asked. They shuffled their feet for a moment and then someone explained that they hadn't believed me about the chillers so they built a room to enclose them. When they turned them on there was a big wind, so they cut holes in the roof to let the air out. I smiled and said that if the chillers still didn't work right, they could cut holes in the walls too.

Downstairs we visited a huge room containing nothing but the emergency generator. The walls were solid; there were no louvers. I suppressed a smile and asked how well the generator worked. They shuffled some more and said that the space got so hot that it shut itself off. I said hm, well, you might try some holes in these walls, too.

Outside, workers mowed lawns, trimmed bushes, swept sidewalks and streets, planted flowers in the center of the entrance drive, for tomorrow was the big day.

And what a day it was! As our car rolled through the gates and a crowd of onlookers, a brass band began playing a cheerful, somehow familiar tune that took a moment to recognize—O Susanna! We laughed with delight.

We joined the big shots and led a procession of hundreds around the grounds. Firecrackers exploded in the trees. The band played. I met the famous CK Hsu from Philadelphia, and directors of institutes around China, and Ministry people from Beijing, and honchos from the Party. The big shots got to stand in the shade on the veranda of the new building, thank goodness, while many speeches were spoken. Someone handed us typewritten translations. Finally the crowd in the hot sun got relief when we paraded through the building, upstairs and down. Smiles on all sides. Then it was across the way into a gymnasium lined with tables, and down to the feast! Course after course, and a small army serving the army of eaters. And the drink! My god, they drank. The toasts didn't stop and the mao tai was strong. When my eyes crossed I refused any more. Toward the end even the servers were staggering, and when we all reeled out after dessert, three or four people stayed behind on the floor.

Driving out of Harbin the next day I had a sudden sensation of jamais vu. Where was I? Where was I in the world, where on earth? Looking over the small valley jammed with brick buildings and corrugated metal roofs jumbled on the hillside spewing black smoke into the cold gray rain, utterly foreign symbols painted on disintegrating fences, filthy, muddy footpaths choked with rubble, dirty people moving randomly, I didn't even know if what I was feeling was life. Had I died and gone to hell? This was followed by a sense of déjà vu: I had been here and knew the place, but couldn't remember where it was. It reminded me of early childhood visits to unknown places, uncomprehended visions of chaos. Then I thought: This place is China. Those are Chinese characters on the crumbling walls. I have travelled far, I am beginning my journey home, to faraway people we have spoken of. When we spoke of them, I imagined them near, but maybe we only imagined them and they don't really exist. Chen Yukun speaks of this and that, and Liu Qing Xiang tells me what he says. But is that what he meant? Does he mean what he says of the friendship between us or does he cynically echo what we say so we will continue assisting his project? The veil and delay of interpretation inhibits engagement with these people the way drink numbs my senses. I think I've lost touch with the world and its people; I am solitary; I've lost touch with my own history, my own web of connections, myself.

But then I told myself not to exaggerate, and chatted with Ella, and gazed at the fields as the outskirts gave way to countryside, and was astonished by a turreted Russian house among the crops and annoyed by Joe monopolizing the conversation. And later I thought, why do I fall in love with places so far from home?

The Getty Museum in LA

The museum treats the spectator as a member of a herd. Admission is free, but arrival is an ordeal. There is no access except the arranged procedure. A shuttle from the parking lot delivers you to stand in a line where people are herded by uniformly t-shirted attendants into the télécabine to the top of the hill, unless you opt to pay a dear bit more for the privilege of parking close and expedited loading onto the lift. Compare this to the Metropolitan Museum of Art or London's National Gallery, both of them free, and both of them a few steps up from the street.

It is clear that with a construction cost of one billion dollars no expense was spared. It is true that the bathrooms are very comfortable and even fitted out with baby wipes. It is true that the Italian travertine is handsome. But the complex was designed by a single person, and it's impossible for a single person to imagine the myriad of interesting details which accrete to places that have been around for centuries.

The buildings are unrelieved by variation or decoration. Why? Perhaps to make the form visible? But the form is unattractive. And given the neo-modernist esthetic, it is surprising to find several columns which serve no structural purpose. The architecture is nonsensical.

Art as spectator sport, art as Disney spectacle. The presentation attempts to impress and intimidate. Security systems pretend to be unobtrusive but are pervasive. The viewer can get no closer than twelve inches to a piece of art. On the other hand, there are computer terminals and screens everywhere; you can get closer to a digital recreation of any piece in the museum than to the piece itself. Art is reduced to flat pixilated images, and though most people raised on Disney probably don't know what they're missing, one would think that a museum billing public education as a goal would make seeing the art itself central to the experience.

The garden is laid out with no sense, no flow and no circulation other than an uncomfortable path down the middle where people must stand aside to let each other pass.

To Idaho with my Son

In August A and I drove to Idaho for a week of camping. No fog there, as there had been all summer in San Francisco, but the forests were burning and the smoke was so thick you couldn't see the mountains.

We came back through eastern Washington and Oregon, a beautiful country of plateaus, rangeland, distant hills, endless empty highways, dirt roads into the dusty and silent boonies. You stop and see sixty vacant miles, a few far-off cattle, the back of an antelope disappearing over a hilltop, a coyote, the constant swish of wind. There is clarity in wide open spaces and in the bare purity of the desert where elemental geology is left uncovered before the blue eye of god. Every motion is accentuated, every feature and every action is framed against the static background of pure form.

With nothing to check them, men's eccentricities flourish and reach extremes unattained in towns. There's nothing to provide perspective, only distance, length, breadth, and the far-off horizon beyond which more hills stretch to mountains somewhere or a peak rising like someone's mania.

Paris in 2005

The Sainte Chapelle is like a Chinese palace, painted as it is in primary red, blue, green and gold.

At mass in Notre Dame Cathedral: Forgive me, Lord, for I'm going to sin. I'm going to take communion.

The metro cars no longer reserve seats for the war mutilated. The mutilated must scramble with the blind, the pregnant, and the old folks for the four labeled seats.

The Latin Quarter has no more couscous; the cheap restaurants are Greek now.

There are still lovers everywhere.

American money shows the faces of crooked politicians. The French shows writers, painters and musicians.

Italian churches are built of circular arches, cylinders, domes and profuse marble; they are light and airy. French churches are of somber stone and high, soaring gothic arches; though stained glass adds color, they are dark.

Jet lag: How bad you feel, how heavy, how the most insignificant problems seem large, how you fixate on things, become obsessed, and are afraid to leave the room. After six days I was in a good mood rather than indifferent or exhausted, but I was not over it. They say it takes a day per hour of derangement. Of course, I've been walking much, much more than usual.

Good old Charlie Hebdo: Television's motto—I don't think, therefore I am.

A Few Days in Umbria with the Family

My father-in-law Frank's wife Sonja is not interested in seeing sights. Frank and I decided last night to visit Assisi today. My wife Wendy was eager and the kids agreed. When Frank told Sonja that he thought we'd all go, she took the news in silence, one of her few silent moments since our arrival.

She talks. Other people are there to listen. Opinions come in the form of questions: "You mean your children won't be able to attend college because you're too well off to get a loan? Isn't that just terrible? How will you pay for them? In Sweden anyone who wants to go, can. Americans just have their values upside down, now don't they? They are so selfish, don't you think?"

Your role is to agree. She is astonished if you don't happen to and is quite put out when gainsaid. But her ideas are not constant. Later she says, "Americans are so friendly and so helpful! So kind and thoughtful, always wanting to make you feel at ease! Don't you think?"

She doesn't speak to me; Wendy is her intermediary. Long after dinner Wendy told me, "Sonja needs your help making a telephone call to Sweden. There's a phone in the bar in Collelungo. Do you mind going? She's really anxious; she's starting to whine."

So I put on my shoes and socks and wait in the kitchen. After several minutes Sonja appears and looks at me silently. I wait for her to state her wishes. Finally she asks awkwardly, "Shall we go?"

Sonja likes Wendy. She has monopolized her. She tells

A Few Days in Umbria with the Family

Wendy about her problems with her son and her parents. She remembers their life in Los Angeles together. Wendy is to listen and respond just enough to get her started on a new topic, but she has to do it subtly so that Sonja thinks she herself changed the subject. This fatigues Wendy.

The kids have both noticed that Grandma doesn't listen to them. My daughter Denise told me that she keeps quiet at dinner because no one talks to her.

Sonja talks about the children in front of them. She is not so indiscreet with grownups unless she can tease them, which she is good at; otherwise she talks about them behind their backs.

She decides how things will be but does not issue direct orders. "I thought the kids would be best in this room and you in that room, but of course you can choose where you want to sleep." Or, "I have bought chicken for dinner tonight. If only I had some bouillon cubes." So off go Wendy and I to Collelungo in search of bouillon cubes. Astoundingly, we find some among the meager offerings of the one store. When we deliver them, Sonja says, "How nice."

Sonja tells Frank what to do and she has begun telling me how to feel. For a few hours I wondered if I should respond to her opinions and sentiments with my own but I realized that she did not want them. I am not expected to respond, though I may make an occasional quip. When Frank makes a pun she lets it pass in silence, displeased that someone else was able to capture the attention for a moment.

My son Sam locked himself into his bathroom. Afterwards Sonja removed the keys from all the bathrooms including ours, which opens only to our bedroom and which nobody but ourselves use. It was a pretext for getting everyone involved in her control mania.

She doesn't want to go to Assisi, so she is still abed at nine AM. Wendy reports that she wants to talk to her sister that evening but is afraid the bar will be closed when we return. Wendy says Sonja has admitted that she works herself up into a state about something and takes it out on others. This self-knowledge and confession hasn't kept her from doing it, though. We must treat her as a child by being calm and mature ourselves, humoring her as far as we care to, but acting as we—not she—choose.

Sonja comes out of her room fifteen minutes later. She looks at the table outside and says, "When we came here, the chairs were all pushed against the table." Wendy understands a command when she hears one so she says, "Like this?" and rearranges the chairs. Sonja, "Yeah, in case of rain, you know."

I expect her to say, "The children aren't ready to go. We can't go until they are ready." I know she won't say, "I must make my telephone call now." She says, "We close the door, don't we?" implying that we others have decided to keep it open. Wendy closes it. Finally we leave for Assisi.

The towns she likes are those with no tourists. She is proud to have discovered this yet undiscovered place where we are staying. It sets her above other people. She is proud of Todi, which has just become chic because a University of Kentucky computer selected it as the best small town in the world. She had the acumen to like it before movie stars and business executives began to buy houses there. (Though had they not bought, she would not be as enthusiastic.) Actually, it was only by chance that this house she rented with Frank's money happens to be nearby.

She likes to think of herself as cultured. "They're not like us, you know. We have educations." But she is transparent. When she describes negative traits in others, she describes herself. "They are so rude… They have no education… no culture… no chic…" She rails against rudeness.

She is venal and grasping. Always talking about Frank's and Wendy's inheritances, Frank's furniture, how Wendy's brother has taken advantage of the family, how unconscionable it is that Wendy's grandfather is not leaving his estate to Denise and Sam (his wife's daughter's divorced husband's children). She has bought herself an apartment in Stockholm with Frank's money and furnished it with his furniture and antique furniture bought from her brother with Frank's money. "I'm an antique collector, you know." When we arrived, she gave us each a bath towel she had thoughtfully brought from England for use around the pool. When we left, she commented that now that the towels were so used up, she would just take the old cast-offs to her apartment in Sweden and buy some nice new ones for her Frank.

This valley of the Tiber between Perugia and Todi is a soft and ordered countryside with rows of alternating tall and short cypress trees. People drive foolishly and selfishly, crowd into lines, and are impatient, though the people in Collelungo are very friendly. It seems familiar, and the cricket and birds and the countryside and frescos of saints' lives seem familiar, not foreign, but they are not mine; they are not of me, nor am I of them. Goethe and Mann assimilated Italy as if it had been their own past, and as Europeans, it was, these buildings, paintings, battles, churches, and they are mine too, though less directly, but I feel a sense of separateness.

Maybe holding myself apart from Sonja's negative craziness keeps me apart from everything else. Wendy, Sonja and Frank have longstanding relationships and are used to each other. Last night Wendy and her father danced and sang off key to taped opera music. I could have wept at the music's beauty, and I almost wept at St Francis's tomb in Assisi, and I did weep at Michelangelo's Pietà. But I felt apart from it all. I feel like an alien who is at home everywhere but not of anywhere. Maybe I assimilate the American way, which is that of the self-sufficient individual who overcomes, or failing that, accepts, but without empathy.

The kids come back from playing. Sonja tells them, "Grandpa was so worried about you. He was afraid you had been hurt." And on and on, trying to make them feel bad about what they've been enjoying. She tries to make everyone feel like they've let someone else down. She says to Frank, "Why is it about you that you worry so much about children?

Weren't you ever a child?" And on and on.

She insists on cooking because it satisfies her sense of injury. The food is tasty and attractively presented, which she points out in case you hadn't noticed, and then she points out that it is immediately destroyed. She creates something fresh, attractive, and original, and others destroy it. The rapid destruction demonstrates yet again (twice daily! without fail!) that others always willfully ruin whatever good she tries to do, proving yet again that she is right to not even try. She makes certain we know we've injured her, which lessens our pleasure as well as her own.

She won't lift a finger to put a dirty dish in the sink. (Which is fine with me; I can get away from the table to do the dishes.) She does nothing to clean up or put things to rights. "Let's hire a cleaning woman."

I ask her for the key to my bathroom. "Oh, there's a whole handful in my room," she says. "Maybe one of them will fit." As if she had just discovered them and hadn't been the one racing around the house pulling them out of the doors. I found the right one and gave her the other three. She turned to Denise and said, "Now what shall we do with these? Put them in this drawer, do you think?" So that she can blame Denise later if it turns out something else should have been done, like putting them back in the doors.

At dinner Denise asks her, "Shall I heat the baked apples?"

"I've already put them in," Sonja replies smugly. "But you can look at them if you want."

Later: alarums and excursions. Sonja shrieks at Denise: "The apples! They're burning! Didn't you take them out?"

Denise told me how much Grandma hurts her feelings. "She was telling me how much more Mom loves me than Sam. That hurt my feelings." She and Sonja had been talking about theater. That is, Denise had talked for a minute or two, calmly and succinctly expressing her feelings and impressions about the experience of acting, and then Sonja discoursed for twenty minutes on the art of acting and the psychology of actors with trite observations such as: Actors act because they are shy and can't get along with people.

"La falsità non dico mai mai, ma la verità non a ognuno." —the Venetian monk Fra Paolo Sarpi, died age 71, born around 1550. "I never never lie, but the truth is not for everyone."

I had the old vertigo of looking up from a fresco in the Ducal Palace and out the window to see the water and the city and not know where I was, and only slowly return to continue telling the fresco's story to Sam, who may or may not have noticed my pause.

The poor boy broke a tooth on a rock that evening and had to wait until we got home to have it fixed.

Wendy and I got along very well. The only bad times were when she vented at me during decompression from the tension of placating Sonja. Sex had never been as good, which made a big difference. But the need to be always on guard with Sonja, to carefully watch what I said so as to never tell a lie but not necessarily the truth, all that vigilance made it harder to share my tender feelings.

Sonja is so relieved that we're leaving that she got royally drunk the second night before our departure. I had gone to San Gimignano, Siena and Florence alone. She had stayed at the house with kids while Frank and Wendy went to Todi for an hour and a half. I returned in time for dinner, to her chagrin—I could tell by the flurry inside as I came up the stairs. I considered leaving to have dinner in town and return later.

She got so thoroughly drunk as the evening wore on that I couldn't stand it and went to the bedroom to do some bookkeeping. Five minutes later I heard her telling Wendy, "Your husband went to bed half an hour ago. He was exhausted."

She cornered me as I went to the kitchen for something. "I can't understand how you can drive all over the Italian countryside and then spend four hours playing with your children. Don't you ever want any time for yourself?"

"It was like going to work, you know. I spent nine hours away and then came home."

"But don't you ever want to be alone? To contemplate things a little?"

I could only smile. I started to explain that the day had been one of contemplation—indeed, I had enjoyed responding to things on my own and hadn't spoken a word of English—I had spent the day alone—but it was no use. She was always for some reason trying to separate Wendy and me from the kids, or at least make us admit that children are indeed demanding and that we wished, even if only for a moment, that they weren't around. She wanted me to agree that yes, my children were nothing but a problem, that I was sick of my wife, my father-in-law and her, that the world had indeed unfairly dealt me a sorry lot.

She said, "I just want to know how you are able to fit into this family." (Her husband's family, I presumed, as I fit well enough into my own, the one here which outnumbered hers by four to two.) "I always like to know how people who marry into it can get along." A theme to which she often returned. "I tried for years to be friendly, treated them like a family, you know, but they never accepted me." Another common theme. "How do you get along?" That was too vague to answer and she was too drunk to understand any rational response.

"Well, whatever works," I said.

She stared at me for a moment and said, "Well, I don't know how you do it." Then she hugged me with a vinous kiss and said, "I really do like you, you know." Probably as apology for the discomfort she's felt around me and the awkwardness she's had in dealing with me as well as forgiveness for my own difficult nature.

"I'm glad," I said as if it made up for seventeen days of cruelty. I had received her blessing. I was OK.

It was a good thing we were leaving the day after tomorrow; we would be lucky if her manic phase lasted that long. Tomorrow's hangover was sure to be unpleasant.

Tehran 2005

I was disoriented most of the ten days I spent in Tehran this July. Although I have been with my Iranian wife and her family and friends for nine years, and seen their snapshots from before the 1978 revolution, and studied Persian literature, architecture, carpets, and handicrafts, and we have translated the poetry of Omar Khayyam, I was unprepared for the taut, energetic and yet warmly personal atmosphere.

My wife, returning for a short visit after thirteen years, our five year old son, her mother, and I were to have spent three weeks there, but my visa application was denied until she spent two weeks going to the Ministry of Foreign Affairs in Tehran, son in tow, while I cooled my heels in Turkey.

I wasn't the only one denied a visa. A Global Exchange tour was forced to visit Lebanon instead, and and Iranian-American friend's daughter, who took a chance traveling without one, had almost been turned back on arrival. We thought we would have better luck because a friend put my wife in touch with a man in the Iranian interests section of the Pakistani embassy in Washington. In February the man said there would be no problem, simply apply to him a few weeks before we wanted to travel. In June, however, after the applications for me and our son had been in for a couple weeks, he said there was a new rule that visa requests had to be made in Tehran. We separated the applications and our son's arrived a week before we left.

We heard several reasons for the policy change. The government was retaliating against the US for denying visas to so many Iranians. There was growing concern about spies.

Presidential elections were approaching and authority was recentralized until the results were known. Ahmadinejad as a candidate had promised to replace four out of five civil servants, and nobody wanted to stick his neck out by letting me in if he was elected.

My wife finally called me in Istanbul to say that the Ministry would fax the approval to their consulate there the next morning and give her an authorization number to give me, but when I arrived the consulate hadn't received it. I found a pay phone two blocks away for the first of many calls about the number. Each time I returned I rang the bell, the inner door opened, the guard scrutinized me, opened the grille, ran a metal detector over me, and asked if I had a knife. They kept saying I should come back tomorrow, but I told them I'd wait since I had a flight at 11:00 that night. My wife's uncle, who lives in Istanbul, gave them a call to let them know I wasn't on my own. I sat in the waiting room trying to sound out Persian words in the magazines and watching Iranian television. Finally they said I was approved; a digit had been missing from the number I had. I filled out a second application, left to pay the fee at a nearby bank, returned with the receipt, and learned that now I needed photos. Out and back again, still without a knife, to watch the janitor clean the empty room. Finally in midafternoon I had the precious visa. I landed in Tehran at 3:30 AM, one of the 500 non-Iranian Americans, including journalists, who visited that year.

One of the journalists was Sean Penn, who wrote a widely published article about his experiences. Mr Penn purposely put himself into troubled situations like political demonstrations and the Friday religious service at Tehran University, which was the primary forum for foreign policy statements, particularly anti-American ones. Unfortunately I didn't have his journalist and star status to help extricate myself from uncomfortable situations, and I had a son who would have suffered if I'd been incarcerated. Mr Penn also had the good fortune to meet people he could identify. I must apologize for not naming or giving significant details about the people

I met. I may be overly cautious, but I don't want to take a chance of jeopardizing anyone.

By way of compensation for my lack of descriptions of political demonstrations, though, I could describe the pain compliance techniques used by our own police on my older daughter and son at a peaceful demonstration here in the good old USA. The police beatings that Mr Penn observed in Tehran happen in San Francisco too.

Don't get me wrong. I enjoyed Mr Penn's reportage more than most since he had few preconceived notions and no viewpoints to project or defend. He was there before the elections; I was there after. The campaign posters had already been removed. The toilets he found noteworthy hadn't changed.

I chose not to attend the Friday religious service at Tehran University. Besides avoiding a problematic situation, my time was taken up with social engagements. We continually saw and received people, some among the national and international business class and some the professional, artistic and academic intelligentsia, some with experience and close contacts in the government, and some ordinary people like myself.

When asked what I thought of Iran, the first word that came to mind was chaos. That was partly due to fragmentary comprehension of a new and unknown place, partly because I had gotten only four hours sleep in the last two nights, and partly because of the heat (over 100 when I finally cleared customs just before sunrise and 117 by evening; the following days peaked at 110), but also because it's chaotic.

The traffic was the first thing I noticed. There seemed to be no rules at all. Then I realized that people drive on the right, most of the time. They slow for stop signs, most of the time. They slow as they approach a blind intersection, unless they're in a hurry. They crowd into any available opening, turn right from the left lane and left from the right. They pull to the side of the freeway and stop; I could never see why.

Eventually I noticed a general practice of accommodation.

To turn onto a busy street, you don't wait for a break in traffic, you nose into it and other drivers let you in. Pedestrians start slowly into the street (anywhere they choose, since traffic lights and crosswalks are far between), and the current separates slightly like water in a shallow, placid river as they wade across. People watch each other. In America, rules are followed; in Iran they are bent. For this to work, everyone must be vigilant. (The ban on alcohol may help raise the level of alertness.) Fortunately most traffic is slow, in part because there is so much of it, but also, I think, because people are in less of a hurry than here. Even the pushiest cabbie sometimes follows a slow car he could easily get around. According to a friend, there are many fender-benders but not serious accidents. On the other hand, two friends of my father-in-law were killed crossing the street.

 Drivers are pushy but don't necessarily insist on their right of way. When a car drifts into their lane, they simply avoid it without the aggrieved honk you would hear here. Horns are used for information: "Watch out, here I am," or "No, I'm not going to let you in." My wife says this is a change—honking used to be constant and universal and self-interest prevailed. There's a story that soon after the revolution a driver asked the cop who stopped him for running a red light, "Why did we have a revolution if we can't ignore traffic lights?"

 People are working out ways of coping with the disorder, but there's a high level of illogical foolishness. One evening we went for dinner at Darband, a small valley heading up into the steep northern hills. The crowded footpath climbs beside a rapid stream surrounded by open-air restaurants, souvenir shops, and vendors selling candied fruit and nuts. Fountains are piped from the stream and water jets in arcs beside the patios under trees strung with lights. Our son stopped to have his fortune told by a parakeet that plucked a *ghazal* by Hafez from a box on a folding table. For an hors d'oeuvre we bought liver *kabab* from two young men tending a charcoal brazier, and later we dined on a platform cantilevered over the stream while our son explored the multi-leveled restaurant, chatting with diners and waiters, indulged by all.

Most people park on the street into Darband before it tapers to a single lane which finally ends at a small parking lot where the footpath begins, but a few insist on seeking a spot as high as they can drive, and when they can't find one they're forced to turn around. A car trying to turn blocks the cars behind, and now a driver coming down stops inches away, blocking it from above. All circulation stops; pedestrians squeeze between the cars. The smell of exhaust, brake fluid, and burning rubber permeates the night. Although no one can move and everyone is suffering, no one honks. Although thoughtlessness and self-interest have generated the condition, there seems to be general acceptance, resignation and patience while it gets sorted out.

The odor of petroleum-based chemicals is pervasive: Car exhaust, gasoline, diesel, transmission fluid, kerosene, fertilizer, plastics, cleansers, shoe polish. Even the dugh (curdled milk) we had with lunch one day in the garden of a palace tasted like chemicals.

Gasoline is imported, surprisingly, because Iran has the world's fourth largest oil reserves. Its refining capacity is small, however; while we were there a refinery opening was celebrated on television. The price of gasoline is subsidized at 40 cents a gallon, which encourages the use of cars. Tehran, like Mexico City, tries to control their number in parts of town at certain times, and to reduce its thick smog the city is beginning a program to buy and scrap 200,000 old cars. A friend pointed out that this also happens to benefit the car manufacturers at taxpayer expense.

Other travelers back from Iran have also described it as chaotic. But let us not exaggerate: Life cannot exist in pure chaos. It's a question of how much there is, and why, and how people cope.

In twenty-five years Tehran grew from two and a half to some fifteen million people. That kind of growth is hard to manage, and there is evidence that the government cares more to maintain its power and enrich its members than to improve conditions for the people it rules.

In order to raise funds, the city has allowed unrestrained building on all available sites. Cranes and building construction are everywhere, but the infrastructure isn't always ready. In a new area at the edge of town, streets between the highrise apartments are merely the ruts left by construction vehicles. In many areas the streets are too small for the traffic. A modern high-speed, automobile-based city is being built on a dense urban grid which cannot accommodate all the vehicles. Buses, which would alleviate the congestion, are infrequent and crowded, and the subway has only two lines.

Only one street map of Tehran is available, and a friend said it is only approximate. Main thoroughfares are shown but smaller streets are not, one-way streets aren't indicated, and apparently continuous streets turn out to be dead ends. Why is this? Mapmakers might have trouble keeping up with newly built streets, but the older ones haven't changed, though many were renamed after the revolution to honor martyrs. Even taxi drivers are unsure of routes and locations. They arrive in the general vicinity and start asking passersby and other drivers where the street is, how to get there from here, and how the numbering works. Sometimes even local shopkeepers don't know.

In a busy part of town, two three-lane one-way streets meet head on, turn a right angle and converge into four lanes. The struggle to reach the streets leading away backs up traffic for blocks.

Left turn lanes direct you into one-way streets coming toward you. At one place, the left turn lane of a six-lane boulevard points directly into traffic leaving our destination on the other side. Since we can't turn there, we're forced to go 500 meters to the next crossing, make a U-turn and return. How did the left turn lane come to be so misplaced?

This all shows a lack of public planning, an absence of controls, a laissez-faire rule. Planning takes discussion, compromise, and agreement. To the extent that it is absent, chaos increases. Many Iranians tell me that they can't get their compatriots to work together, but at the same time a great deal of energy is being put into civil society efforts—which the government supports up to a point. One of our friends is organizing a wildlife and camping society, and its mere existence, he said, will be subversive, since people will gather on their own and make their own rules. There is much talk in US foreign policy these days of democracy building; we would do better to talk about consensus building.

Maybe so much growth in such a short time is uncontrollable. Maybe the best cities have developed like this and smoothed their rough edges when expansion slowed. Istanbul, New York, and London have good public transportation, room on the streets, shops within walking distance, public spaces; they are comfortable places now, but consider their past unrestricted growth. And consider how cold are planned cities like Frankfurt, Brasilia, and La Défense in Paris, and how much a "planned society" smacks of twentieth century totalitarianism. Maybe a crazy place like Tehran has a better chance than Frankfurt of becoming comfortable, since its development springs from the diversity of individual choices. I suppose we can't help analyzing and prescribing, but in the end our theories and prescriptions may count for little. People develop and adapt on their own.

Tehran feels like a war zone, a chaos where rules are suspended, self-interest governs, and decent people carry on their lives as best they can. My Russian piano teacher has described her childhood during the siege of Leningrad and life under Stalin. It's one thing to hear about and another to visit. The ruling mafia prosecuted a war with Iraq just after the revolution and they have found methods for maintaining the atmosphere. Anxiety and fear serve the purposes of certain governments, like the Chinese Cultural Revolution and the American War on Terror.

I learned a few things about America on this trip. The

US is becoming more like Iran in its use of fear to create an obedient populace. Look at recent developments: Nonsensical airport security measures, colored terror alerts, corporations looting pension funds, HMOs denying proper care to patients, NAFTA and CAFTA moving jobs out of the country, manufacturers making shoddy and unsafe products, underfunded schools and libraries, the huge number of African-American and Hispanic males in prison.

In Tehran, public behavior is more restricted than in the US. Men and women cannot shake hands. Women must cover their hair. They must wear drab clothing at government offices—my wife was refused entry to the Ministry of Foreign Affairs when she wore pants that were too colorful.

We attended a concert in the walled garden of Niavaran Palace, once used by the shahs. To one side was a lovely 19th century traditional pavilion and behind the stage was a 20th century palace in High Commercial style. Since women are not allowed to sing unaccompanied by a man, one of the men had cultivated the trick of singing so as to be barely audible. Imagine how much effort has been wasted to cope with this particular restriction. Before the revolution Tehran had a good opera company. Not now—how many operas have only male roles?

There is evidence of a mean and vicious streak. The customs people who processed me at the airport were rude and one bordered on malicious. Now and then unshaven men with untucked shirts would stare at us with hostility in the street, though normally they ignored us as we ignored them. People talked about beatings and detentions of students and journalists, and Akbar Ganji's hunger strike in Evin Prison was closely followed.

The random brutality of state-sanctioned violence charges even casual outings. One night as we left the city to drive over the hill for dinner in Zardeband, traffic crawled through a checkpoint. We were waved through, but the unshaven men searched other cars for alcohol.

As we sped up, our driver, an Iranian friend who had

recently moved back after twenty years in Los Angeles, joked that the lack of lane markers on the freeway actually improves circulation since everyone can move anywhere as traffic conditions change. He mentioned that it had taken him six months to grow moderately comfortable with local traffic.

Near the town limits of Zardeband we drove through an unmanned checkpoint. After dinner, where the use of video cameras was forbidden and women were not allowed to smoke *qaliyun* (water pipe)—though they smoked cigarettes nonstop like the men—we passed the checkpoint in the other direction. Now it was manned in glaring light, and a group of untucked shirts surrounded three or four young men and women with their hands on heads. There was dismay in our car as they told me the kids faced lashings and months in prison. I wondered why they had been so foolish as to carry alcohol in the car.

According to a friend in a position to know, the church masters in Qom were not particularly well organized before the revolution. But they are very smart, and they went to the Vatican to learn how the Catholics minister their own flock. Now there is a computerized database of clerics in the villages, the cities, the neighboring countries, and around the world. (This friend also described his vision of the Middle East as a region which during the day is zoned into the countries of Iraq, Iran, Afghanistan, Tajikistan, Syria and so on, but at night is a fluid, borderless network of people and goods moving along paths ordered by different rules.)

The government allows intellectual culture as long as it is discreet. They must, after all, allow some interchange of thought to keep things running, but they control the level at which things are permitted to run. The lack of planning, the level of violence, and the amount of chaos are generally assumed to be premeditated and calibrated. The leaders promote the popular culture which supports them and they have also chosen to promote religious fundamentalism. For example, a Bachelor's degree can be had for memorizing the Koran. Puritan Islamic repression, though implemented more thoroughly in Iran, is of the same nature as the fierce Christian fundamentalism in America and serves the same political ends.

It is commonly accepted that if you don't know your contractor you can't expect decent or even safe construction. Much of the masonry tile being used for walls seemed to be of poor quality. A contractor we know was not even sure if there are building codes. He did point out a highrise, though, where construction had been halted until structural calculations were redone and more steel added.

My wife's aunt's apartment building was built before the revolution and is therefore considered trustworthy. Recently, though, a woman bought the small ground floor apartment and enlarged it by removing a column. When cracks appeared in our aunt's and other tenants' walls, someone complained to the building department. The woman bribed the inspector they sent with money or sex, nobody knew for sure. Our aunt asked my mother-in-law what she thought about trying to unite the tenants to appeal, but they decided that the most she could achieve would be a fine of a couple thousand dollars (which would not be distributed to the tenants), the column would not be replaced, and the woman's engineer's reputation for accomplishing tricky jobs would be enhanced.

They told me there's really no civil remedy available. I didn't learn more, but it's clear that where shame is absent and law is not valued there is little to check acts of greed and cruelty. We see this trend here, where our rights as individuals to sue corporations are being diminished.

Not everyone is happy with the repression, and rebellion takes whatever form it can. As time goes by, scarves creep from the brow to the top of the head. Women color their hair, make up their faces, and wear stylish shoes. The young ones wear tall platforms and make their drab overcoats into tight cocoons that reveal their shapes. Certainly their fathers and brothers and husbands support this, for they couldn't push so far alone. They are at the forefront and it could be that it's they who finally bring down this government.

The history of the Middle East, and the world in general, is the patient creation of order and beauty followed by its destruction in war after war after war. A history of brutality and theft and of small groups in the gaps creating calm, civilized oases as best they can. Culture and intellect require leisure, but leisure does not necessarily lead to cultivation of the intellect: In America it has led to the commodification of everything. (Consequently American intellectuals seek to create value in the face of banality—the rest of the world refines value from chaos.)

At a family gathering where beer and vodka were freely drunk with the full consent of the host despite his strong Islamic belief, a young second cousin who is studying French at the university asked for my impressions of Iran. I told her it seems that there are two societies living in parallel with little contact, the cultured one hidden from the other. "Yes," she agreed, and added, "Many more than two."

The thoughtful, graceful culture that I had expected does live. It is indoors, behind garden walls, in the apartments and houses, concealed in small enclosed spaces, where order and safety are found. There is the life of the mind, of friendship and family, where men and women kiss cheeks upon greeting, news of the world is as fresh as today, books are discussed, art and craftsmanship are prized.

Even popular culture includes the classics. Lines from Khayyam are woven into carpets. Ordinary people know his poetry by heart. Fortunes are told by opening a collection of Hafez's poetry at random. Our son bought another fortune from a street vendor—another verse by Hafez. Shakespeare is not so current among us.

People speak with quick wit and irony, without cynical affectation. Strangers would walk up and ask where I was from, which often led to frank and interesting conversations. You can say anything you want, though once my wife thought it prudent to tell a revolutionary guard that I was from Canada.

She later felt bad about that and from then on we owned up to the truth. Nobody cared.

We headed for the bazaar one morning with a childhood friend and her son. Women board the buses through the rear door and sit at the back. The boys were young enough to go with them but I had to squeeze my way from the front door to the low bar that separated us. No one talked to us although they listened attentively to our English and Persian. On the subway a young man struck up a conversation in halting English and talked all the way up to the sidewalk.

The bazaar is an immense collection of narrow covered pedestrian streets, two or three stories high with shops at ground level, fans and air conditioners jutting overhead, surmounted by a skylit roof. Shops are grouped by what they sell—jewelry, carpets, hardware, food. We took a passageway to the outside past a mosque with a beautiful blue-tiled dome, crossed the courtyard, and entered another area where less expensive jewelry and stones were sold. In a small tearoom men sat side by side behind small tables offering bracelets, rings, necklaces, pendants and tea as we looked at their wares. They smiled and mussed our son's hair. At another shop we bought bugles for the boys, the kind of noisemaker you find at sports events. We admonished the boys not to blow them in the crowded surroundings but everyone smiled and surreptitiously encouraged them. We bargained a little over price but generally paid what was asked, figuring that a few extra dollars would help them much more than it would hurt us.

In some countries touts and beggars follow you down the street, but not in Iran. People respect themselves too much for that kind of self-abasement. In fact, it happened only one time, in the bazaar, where a man insisted that we look at his carpets, that the shop we were headed for was overpriced, and that our friend, who was leading the way, would be getting a commission on whatever we bought, and, by the way, were we sure that she was truly a friend? We laughed hard at that.

Not that sellers won't take advantage of you—if someone can overcharge you he will, and I heard plenty of stories of dishonest transactions. Dishonesty is not hypocrisy though, and I'd rather deal with frank dishonesty than smug pretense. Even the few beggars are dignified as they patiently await alms.

Back in the US, it took me weeks to readapt to the pervasive reticence and fear. Here in the US nobody meets your eye on the street, no one smiles or greets you. This is a place where children are taught not to speak to strangers and grownups are afraid you might ask them for something. Everyone is afraid of one thing or another. Afraid of losing their job, afraid of black people, afraid of walking after dark, afraid terrorists will sneak over the border and strike the shopping mall, afraid their kids aren't being well enough educated, afraid of sex, afraid of the right-wing conspiracy or the left-wing. People won't talk about politics, their salary, their boss. I speak of the educated white middle class, of course. The grandchildren of the slaves may be wary, but they're not fearful.

Iranians are generous. We went to a bank one afternoon so my wife could pay the fee to leave the country. When a woman in line saw that the clerks (all men) ignored her, she energetically demanded the forms we needed and then took the time to explain how to complete them. A few minutes later, a young couple turned disappointed from the counter as they realized they would have to return home to get the bit of money they lacked for their own exit visa. Another woman, a stranger, insisted that they accept the money from her.

Tehran has trees, public gardens, and well-equipped children's playparks. Channels called *jubs* carry running water alongside many streets, left over from the days (less than fifty years past) when they were the city's water supply. Once a week the residents of each block met to channel the water into their cisterns. Now water is piped but the jubs irrigate the trees and delight with their sight and sound.

Our son had a great time. Of course, he was the son of a beloved friend who was visiting after many years and a relative of many we met, and his sociability brings out the best in everyone; but more than that, Iranians treat children with affection and indulgence.

His lack of inhibition worried me now and then, as when he flopped on the floor of a shop to act like he was praying. He did this more than once. I keep forgetting to ask him why, but he probably doesn't know himself. He did like the azan (call to prayer) sung five times a day. Certainly he's too young to be sardonic, but I worried that someone would think he was making fun of something they hold dear. No one ever seemed to react, though.

He took swimming lessons at a nearby daycare center so he'd meet other children and get some relief from the heat. The teachers were all kind and attentive young women, in hejab of course. The children were cheerful and friendly and played well together. Although none were older than six, separate lessons were held for boys and girls in the small pool in the garden.

One afternoon we visited friends in an apartment building with a pool. Our friend mentioned that during the winter, men and women use the indoor pool at different times, and in summer women use the indoor and men the outdoor. After buying tickets at the building office, we strolled in the shade under the trees enjoying the whiff of kerosene in the air. A woman in hejab tended the garden in the heat. The pool was screened from the path by a hedge and my wife had to stop short of the opening so that she wouldn't see the men in their swimming suits.

My son and I were clearly foreigners and English speakers, and I had no idea how this would be received. Presumably the swimmers were building residents—upper class, professional and educated—but these mostly unshaven men didn't seem particularly cosmopolitan. However, though they checked us out, they didn't stare.

Nobody talked to us. Everyone was subdued. There was no play, no splashing, no laughter. The men—there were no children—talked quietly in small groups. One spectacularly muscled middle-aged man who swam well gave pointers to a respectful young man. Four or five teenagers lounged at the edge in a self-absorbed group. I was uncomfortable. The air of restraint and inhibition was unsettling, and there were no women. Groups of only men make me uneasy because of their tendency to uninhibited aggression. That may be peculiarly American, but I suspect that all authoritarian patriarchal societies condone and provoke male violence, particularly against outsiders.

My son pointed out that the bottom was dirty. There was also dirt and trash around the benches, hedges, and corners. As soon as I reasonably could, I suggested that we leave. The changing room floor was slimy. We left for the clean, welcoming camaraderie inside the apartment.

Our friend rued the building's shabbiness. His parents had lived there since before the revolution, when apartments belonging to members of the Shah's cabinet and other prominent people were confiscated and given to families of martyrs, men from the south of Tehran or the countryside killed in the war with Iraq. The new people pretty much trashed the place and later sold their apartments, but after twenty-five years some remained. All these years the building had been poorly maintained. Our friend had been encouraging members of the tenants association to contribute three thousand dollars per apartment for repairs and upgrades to the elevators, lobbies and common areas, but no one trusted anyone. People feared that the person in charge would take the money or that it would be unwisely spent. He couldn't convince them that the value of their apartments was dropping and that unless repairs were made things would become irreparable.

Much about America is admired around the world—its popular culture, consumer goods, its former democracy and generosity—though this is rapidly changing as it becomes an empire. A cultivated, thoughtful lady who spends part of her year in Canada and part in Tehran working in her family's business told us that visiting us at home would be difficult, because her Canadian passport reflects her origins and she is not welcomed at the border. When we pressed her to find a way to come, she said that as much as she likes us, she dislikes the US too much to visit. Another friend had enough of the US at college in Denver, and though she has friends and family in the US would rather spend her vacations elsewhere.

Having heard Americans speak disparagingly of foreign places they've traveled, it was refreshing to have a few foreigners return the favor. This summer I happened to visit Jordan, France, Turkey, and Iran, and I talked with people from still other places. People everywhere are well informed about the world and the US, and we would do well to listen to their comments.

Travel is a wonderful thing. You get away from the grind, see beautiful things, and acquire new perspectives. In Europe and North America toilets are fixtures with a seat seventeen inches above the floor and a roll of paper nearby for wiping. In the Middle East they are a hole in the floor bracketed by two platforms for your feet and a faucet or hose nearby for cleansing. Some Americans find this risible and primitive. An Indian friend says that in her mother's opinion, civilization, in its course from India westward, ends at Greece, where water is no longer plumbed beside the toilet and people are forced to use that unsanitary paper.

The New California Academy of Sciences Museum

There is only one public entrance, on the north side where the scant parking costs money. There is ample parking, and free, on the south, but you have to walk all the way around the building. On the east you must walk through a planted area or across grass, and the paved path on west runs along an unattractive service road. The old south entrance has been replaced by one for employees only. Too bad they don't at least let you exit there; it would save a long walk.

The museum is loaded with interesting architecture. Interesting, but not graceful. Monumental, but not comfortable, though there are lovely views of the architecture from everywhere and good views of the surrounding park from the balcony and bridge on the second floor. Good views, but only one stair in the center; when you explore, you have to walk all the way back. But the building is handsome, well lit and spacious.

The high white sphere of the planetarium looming over the eating court is balanced on the other side by the transparent sphere containing a tropical rain forest. Superstar architect Renzo Piano originally wanted the transparent sphere to be filled with fish but the engineers told him it wouldn't hold water, so he made it a terrarium. I wonder whether he considered the effect of a sphere of water towering unnaturally overhead, or how to keep its bottom clear of detritus.

We miss the endless rooms off rooms of the old museum, filled with exhibits and new collections that surprised us when we poked into a room we had forgotten or passed in our haste to revisit a favorite display.

We miss the rock collection and the pickled coelacanth.

We very much miss the old diorama with sound and light that recreated a day and night on the African savannah, the roar of lions, the thunderstorm, the chirping of birds and muttering of primates. It was probably an anachronistic concoction of events and animals, but it was a wonderful experience.

The alligator pit reuses the lovely old wrought iron railing to keep people from falling in, and introduces carbon dioxide vapor above the water where the alligators and turtles breathe. It's good opera, the swamp as spectacle, and undoubtedly has more verisimilitude than the old diorama.

The old aquarium had tank after tank filled with fish; the new one has a few small tanks in the wall with graphics in between. The tidepool is larger. Alas, the fish swimabout is no more; gone is the charm of being surrounded by fish swimming eternally, eternally visible in the dim light.

We miss other small, fun, simple things about the old museum, like the hyperbolic funnel that rolled your coin down into the donation box, the clatter and shuffle of feet on the floor, the feeling that you could never see all the exhibits, there were so many, the glassed-in displays you could press your nose against.

The Museum as Education

The experience of unusual natural things is no longer unmediated. Informative, interactive electronic displays are everywhere. Guess the carbon footprint of the french fries and pizza you eat. Learn about global warming and climate. Watch the various species arrive at the Galapagos Islands. Be apprised that a roller coaster company designed and built the ramp inside the terrarium.

Behind plate glass windows the workings of science are displayed. Paying guests may spend an afternoon at the CAS learning how to dissect birds, which, a sign explained (no doubt to allay concerns about vivisection), have been found dead by the roadside. (Or from having flown into the huge exterior windows?) Under the direction of CAS staff the sciento-tourists in white smocks and latex gloves work at several tables, one equipped with an expensive microscope and computer. They learn how to make the cuts and pin the specimens to boards. The apprentice surgeons are careful not to meet the eye of the public on the other side of the glass. The public is mildly revolted. But it's good to know how science functions, that it involves cutting things up, and if it may not be in the best of taste to do so publicly, that's the tough reality of it.

THE MUSEUM AS COMMERCE

Admissions is $25/adult, $10/child, $15/youth. Maybe that's why you see no black faces and few brown ones apart from the Latino servants in the cafeteria. You wonder how the few working class people that you spot could swing the cost. (Seven years later the costs are $35/$25/$30. Compare these to $18/$13/$15 at Chicago's Field Museum. What's Chicago doing that San Francisco is not?) (And why do these affluent visitors need so many security guards?)

There are three eating places. You can buy sandwiches in the old outdoors quad, now a soaring glass-enclosed square, where once you ate the sandwiches you brought with you. There is a celebrity chef-inspired cafeteria. There is a premium private lounge with catering and bar service up an elevator.

There are three retail shops: the main gift shop, the aquarium gift shop, and the children's shop.

THE MUSEUM AS ENTERTAINMENT

Computer games for children. Catch the bugs, catch the butterflies. For the younger kids, stomp on the bugs, see them rush under leaves for protection.

Evenings out for young adults. Be a Night Life VIP. For $59, cocktails included, of course, you go behind the scenes, listen to a rock band or a dj, meet other young, single (or maybe not) adults in your income bracket.

The Museum as Roof

The stair leads up to a very small viewing platform from which little can be seen: the squat brown De Young Museum across the concourse—which given the angle of sight is only partly visible—the elevator enclosure, and the semi-spherical mounds on the so-called living roof which represent the seven hills of San Francisco, a local attempt at self-identification with the seven hills of Rome. We imagine architect Piano's presentation to the CAS board of directors about mapping San Francisco's topography onto the building, thus reifying their conceit that the city partakes of eternal Rome's spirit.

The viewing platform is enclosed by a fence with emergency egress gates that swing open when pushed; signs warn against leaning on them. My son happened to bite his tongue badly as we stood there, and we both leaned against the closest thing, a gate, so he could recover and I could examine the damage. The gate began to swing and a polite but firm security guard approached to shoo us away.

The seven mounds do not please the eye, and a regular array of small circular skylights marches across the roof without regard for them. Seen from the huge space below, the light is great, but from where we stand the skylights are symmetrical artificialities in geometrically perfect bumps whose artificiality gives the lie to the supposed organic nature of the roof.

It is covered with grass and weeds native to the region. Chicken wire covers gravel-filled channels that bring runoff to hidden drains. Too bad the chicken wire was not mapped to show the route of the 49-mile drive which visitors can take among the real hills.

The old museum, and others of its ilk like the Field Museum and New York's American Museum of Natural History, was a neoclassical building with comfortable grand rooms that merely contained its exhibits. The visitor peacefully contemplated the collection without background distractions. Nowadays we value sustainable buildings, natural lighting, and a sense of the surrounding world, but our post-modern designers sometimes forget that a building and its accoutrements should serve its function. But maybe this one does. What after all is its function? The ambience we have here quite suits the museum as idea of museum.

A Couple Days in San Diego

We drove down to Border Field State Park in the Tijuana River estuary next to the Mexican border. The river bottom and hills are very arid with greasewood, horse stables, dust, and military helicopters practicing in low, noisy circles. As you get closer you can see the old fifteen-foot high border wall of dark brown solid metal. It never did a great job keeping the Mexicans out, so on this side a new wall is being built of twenty foot high, ten inch diameter concrete piers spaced three or four inches apart, too narrow for a person to squeeze through, said my brother, who supplies material to a subcontractor to Kiewit, the general contractor building this section. My dad wanted to drive up to the Kiewit yard to look at the equipment but my brother said no, he didn't want anybody to see him and point him out when he came back in a few days for work. We didn't see anybody anywhere.

The gate across the entrance road to the park was shut and a sign said it was open on weekends and holidays. Today being neither, my dad turned the car onto a dirt road by the barricade, figuring we could drive around it through the brush. This place will be swarming with cops in five minutes, I said. Good thing my skin isn't too dark, my Iranian wife said. Our eight year old son wanted to know what we were talking about.

It took all of two minutes for the first Immigration and Customs Enforcement patrolman to arrive, standing on his all-terrain vehicle in his neat green uniform with pockets and belts, helmeted and armed, and a tough, overfed face. What are you headed off to do, he demanded. We're going up to Border Field Park, my dad said. It's closed, the ICEman said. Nice of ICE, I thought, to be guarding parks for the State of California. Another one arrived on another ATV. I wondered how far dad was going to push it. He chewed on his tongue for a moment and then said okay. We headed back. The ICEmen didn't follow. I don't suppose they had to; they could see our dust and I'm sure they had other means of surveillance.

In the old days the cops and the military showed a certain amount of gruff courtesy when they gave you orders—at least to us white folks—a certain generosity grounded in the crude and brute force they exercise. But those were days of victory and success, when noblesse obliged and there was scope for some individual exercise of discretion. You could negotiate a little leniency. In these days of failure, defeat, and unemployment, when cruelty and oppression are sanctioned at the highest levels, that largesse is squelched. Now they're all mean and nasty; nor do they care, or dare, to act independently.

The entire San Diego area feels like a military camp. Or maybe like occupied territory. That is, for us peaceable civilians. Around here it looks like you're either in the military or working for it, and if you're not they'd like you to think they're protecting you. From what? Mexicans for one thing, I guess. And terrorists. From yourself, maybe—if you're a civilian then you can't be totally trusted, and you've got to be controlled to protect them, or you, or something—or am I being paranoid? It's a weird place, gives me weird thoughts.

Maybe statistics would prove me wrong, but the economy feels like a military economy. The major things you see being manufactured and built are border walls and military facilities. You see battleships and carriers in the bay, bases and naval air stations along the freeways, soldiers in camouflage sitting in the backs of trucks or on gates in fences at freeway exits in the countryside with nothing around, tattoo parlors and strip joints on the main streets of National City, Imperial Beach, Chula Vista, the immense retired officers community of Coronado, jeeps and Humvees and SUVs on the highways, black with tinted windows, like the ones driven by special forces around the world, driven here by young men with buzz cuts and wraparound sunglasses or thin young women with frizzy hair, or not so thin with a back seat full of buzz-cut boys in camouflage T-shirts.

Besides the black jeep-like vehicles there are pickup trucks. Pickups are driven by the ruggedest individuals, the cowboys, the construction workers, the men who move things, the not-sissies, the ones who don't think and don't need to think and despise thinking. They're driven by single young men or occasionally by a big-breasted young woman in a tight shirt, haughty because it's her boyfriend's pickup.

There's a lot of testosterone. Strip joints, pickup trucks, crew cuts, tattooed biceps in sleeveless T-shirts. Tough sneers. Expressionless faces. Hostility.

We saw a van with quite a paint job: An eagle, red white and blue streamers, and text that announced "For God. For the Flag. For the Marines." Me, I pray to God and the Flag that it belonged to a Marine recruiter and not a civilian. It was bad enough for a recruiter, but if it was civilian, there's a real nutcase driving around.

Aggressive driving, cutthroat, give no quarter. Two cars behind me pull into an off-ramp on my right. They both speed up at once but the one behind is faster and crowds the other. They just miss my bumper as they accelerate toward the red light at the end of the ramp. They must be test pilots. Lots of them on the roads here.

Mulish driving. Somebody pulls into the leftmost lane to pass someone going marginally slower and then stays there although he's holding back a line of cars in the fast lane. He's there, he's going the speed limit, the rest of the world can damn well get over it. Further north, in LA for example, people who do this are simply oblivious or on the phone or spacing out to their iPod, but people here are ornery. If you don't believe me, try getting around the guy by pulling into a break in the lane to his right. He speeds up to keep you there until you come up on the next car and have to slow down;

then he slows down.

There are many poor people. They look miserable and beaten down. It's depressing. They're fat, they wear shoddy clothes, they frown. The blacks are unhappy and solitary, the Mexicans are quiet, and the whites swagger around in their fatness, feeling good that they're the bosses, the top of the heap, the ones all the stores are for, the flags and the soldiers and fighters in far-off Afghanistan or Syria or wherever freedom needs fighting for. You see them in the discount stores, not the chain outlets in the malls, but the ninety-nine cent grocery stores, the bulk grocery discount stores, the places that sell day old bread and canned vegetables and styrofoam containers of flavored pasta just add water, the stores that sell bad food cheap enough for these poor people to buy.

Go close to the border fence and look at poor people on the Mexican side—the kids are running and playing, the grownups are sitting or standing around chatting, vendors stroll up selling one thing or another. This side looks like a DMZ, except it isn't demilitarized, it's militarized. You can't have a social life with ICEmen and military helicopters. Take a look at the fence. It looks like bars on a jail; the question is who's in and who's out?

Look through the fence but don't bother crossing the border. Easy enough leaving, but coming back—hoo boy!—that's another story. Two hours standing in line or sitting in a car or on a bus waiting to show your passport. Ain't worth it. Somebody doesn't want us fraternizing with the enemy. Or seeing what we're missing. Or maybe they figure we'll gladly pay this small price of time for protection against the aliens.

Unfriendly people here. You can't meet anyone. Usually poor people are less uptight than affluent ones, but here they are silent and sullen. You can't get close to the affluent ones in their cars, factory outlet shopping malls, and suburban houses. Now and then you will encounter someone at the zoo or a nature interpretive center but they won't meet your eye, they won't return your smile, and they often won't even acknowledge a spoken hello. The friendliest among them only smile briefly before glancing away. It's worse than being in an elevator because there at least you know it's etiquette. Here people don't know how to act. Everybody in the county is shy, I guess, or they're afraid of acting friendly first and not having the gesture reciprocated or of being tricked into smiling back at a con man. They're afraid of something.

I used to dread being around other tourists because their jolly camaraderie got on my nerves. "Where you from?" with a big smile. "Mom and me, we're from Decatur, staying down at the beach at an RV campground. Great place this California. Where you staying?" I hate it. But now I think it may be better than the studied lack of contact there is now. People don't meet your eye, the white people, the big open-hearted Americans who used to camp around the world.

The US has a tradition of disdain and even disgust for elite privilege, militarism, authoritarian rule. Maybe people will start rebelling against the twenty year old trend the other way. It would be one of few such historical occurrences, but it might be possible given our more or less widespread training in civic activities. We *could* reject small-mindedness and instead cultivate cheerfulness, generosity, and sociability.

On the other hand, the US also has a mean streak, a tradition of immigrant-hating know-nothingness, a conquer-and-take frontier attitude. We share in the human affinity for rapine and cruelty. Apocalyptic me: It seems like the mean streak has won. Hostility reigns. The sky is low and heavy, there's no space to breathe, no room for friendship with strangers. A rebellion of the good-minded isn't going to happen around here soon.

Think about all the returning soldiers and contractors and depatriating allies from around the empire. They know how to obey and how to command. They know police work. They know security. They need jobs, and it so happens there are plenty of jobs in immigrant control and antiterrorism and the prison system and shopping center security. A lot of these jobs are in San Diego, and a lot of soldiers started their service here and liked the place enough to return, so the military attitude of the place is no surprise.

I can just hear some of the reactions to this piece: "Go back where you came from, a**hole!" Me: "I'm from here, dude. I got nowhere else to go."

Or: "Love it or leave it." Me: "Right. Ain't a lot better elsewhere. Same goddamned aggressive patriotism, same aggressive religionification, same merchandizing, same lies, same fraud."

Man, in the old days at least the conquerors didn't lie. Rape and pillage were straightforward. Don't get me wrong, I don't yearn for the days of the Vandals and the Horde. Things are better now than ever for peaceful types like me. No question. And civilization has always been made in the corners away from the big shots and the thugs. But I do hate the abounding lies these days.

You want an example? They tell us we the people are in charge. They give us the illusion of control on billboards that advertise: My Television. My Rules. That is, control the channels your child can watch. Lie #1: If you own it you control it. Lie #2: Control is good. Lie #3: Ownership is good. Lie #4: Television is good. Lie #5: Influence comes from ownership, not anything like example or discussion. Lie #6: You own your children. Lie #7: You're in control. Of your life! Of your kids! You be da boss! Big shot! You! Never mind you got no say where you work, you might even gonna lose your job you got no idea, the price of gas goes up, people buy fewer cars, you get laid off from making windshield wiper blades. Solly, Cholly. You can get retrained at the University of Phoenix to become a middle manager. Or go home and control your TV! Not to mention the self-centered, smug, bossy tone: Nyah, nyah, nyah, it's my ball so you gotta play by my rules. They want you to act like the kid everyone hates.

The trouble is, you can't talk to people about this. They're either naïve or complicit. You make the naïve ones uneasy and they cut you off or repeat the day's party line at you, and they usually get hostile. The complicit ones are hostile from the get-go. These days hostility is the modus operandi of the

Bushies, the neocons, our friends in the Middle East, and the others in control. In days gone by, you ignored gadflies. These days you swat them. These days are vicious. Some people—poor people especially—know this already but what can they do? What good does talking about it do? You can't teach the naïve, can't convert the complicit, can't expect poor powerless saps like us to be able to do anything. I guess you talk about it so a few like-minded people know they're not alone.

www.ingramcontent.com/pod-product-compliance
Lightning Source LLC
LaVergne TN
LVHW091302080426
835510LV00007B/360